YORKSHIRES
REAL·HERITAGE·PUBS

Pub Interiors of Special Historic Interest in Yorkshire and Humber

REVISED EDITION

Edited by **David Gamston**

CAMPAIGN
FOR
REAL ALE

Based on CAMRA's Yorkshire Regional Inventory of Historic Pub Interiors

Produced by CAMRA's Pub Heritage Group
www.heritagepubs.org.uk
info.pubheritage@camra.org.uk
With support from CAMRA Books:
Simon Hall, Katie Button and Emma Haines.

Published by the Campaign for Real Ale Ltd
230 Hatfield Road, St Albans,
Hertfordshire AL1 4LW
www.camra.org.uk/books

© Campaign for Real Ale 2014

First Published 2011
Reprinted with updates and amendments 2011
Revised edition 2014

ISBN 978-1-85249-315-8

A CIP catalogue record for this book is available from
the British Library

Printed and bound in the United Kingdom by
Cambrian Printers Ltd, Aberystwyth.

Maps/floorplans: Stephen Bere; (Ray Balawajder page 51)

Book design/typography: Dale Tomlinson

Photo credits
Photographs © Michael Slaughter LRPS, apart
from the following;
(Key: t=top, b=bottom, m=middle, l=left, r=right)

Front cover and Pages 16, 20(b), 64(r), 74, 75(m),
   76(r), 79, 82(ml), 86(b), 87 – Paul Thompson
Pages 1, 13(t), 22(b), 29(bl), 34(t), 35(bl), 35(br),
   38, 47(r), 48, 82(mr), 83(t), 83(br) 86(t) –
   Geoff Brandwood
Pages 12, 26, 30(l), 33(t), 35(t), 36(t), 89(b) –
   Allan Sykes
Pages 13(b), 69(t), 88(b) – John Thornton
Pages 15(b), 17, 18(m), 20(t), 28, 36(b), 37, 43(mr),
   46(tr), 49(t), 54(tl), 54(tr), 56(ml), 61(mr), 62,
   67(b) – Dave Gamston
Pages 21(t), 73 – Paul Dixey
Page 29(t) – by permission of Pam Eldred
Page 33(br) – by permission of Barrie Pepper
Page 42 – Peter Carlton
Page 45(ml) – Amanda Wilkinson
Pages 46(mr), 46(bl), 46(br) – Stuart Mumby
Page 51(r) – Melissa Reed
Page 55(m) – Richard Brown
Page 56(t) – Paul Crossman
Page 57(mr) – Will Forrest
Page 64(l) – Paul Ainsworth
Pages 65(b), 67(m) – Laurie Wilson
Page 67(r) – Chris Dixon
Page 81(ml) – by permission of Sarah Whitelock

Cover and title pictures
Front cover: the vaults at the Garden Gate, Leeds
Back cover: main bar at the White Horse ('Nellie's'),
   Beverley
Page 1(title page): counter-screen detail at the
   Coach & Horses, Barnburgh
Page 2 (this page): window detail at the Old Cock,
   Halifax

Contents

Introduction **Pubs to Cherish**

Yorkshire's Real Heritage Pubs lists the 119 public houses in the Yorkshire region which still have interiors or internal features of real historic significance. They are a richly-diverse part of Yorkshire's cultural and built heritage. Some of them, indeed, are treasures of national stature and most are a joy to visit.

Worrying numbers, however, are closed or for sale at the time of going to press (enough, in fact, for us to show a special symbol in our listings). Some, perhaps, may never re-open. For in Yorkshire, just as elsewhere in Britain, pubs are going out of business at an alarming rate and the great tradition they represent is under threat as never before. The uncertain world of market forces, in which our pubs have to survive, is now made so much worse by the present harsh economic climate, by loopholes in our planning laws, by tax burdens, by unfair competition from supermarkets and, for many pubs, by the demands of the modern-day pub companies.

No pub, however historically rare, is guaranteed a safe future. What is also painfully true is how few authentic old pub interiors have been able to survive the tidal wave of modernising change that took hold from the mid-1960s onwards. Our guide's 119 entries are a mere 2 percent of Yorkshire's total pub stock (of around 6,000) and the need to safeguard the little we have left has become a pressing conservation challenge.

The dwindling of our pub heritage has gone largely ignored by mainstream conservationists and it has fallen to CAMRA to fill the gaps, both of knowledge and of serious preservation effort. Yorkshire has played a major, pioneering part in CAMRA's initiatives but, until 2011, when the first edition of this booklet was launched, there had been no published guide to the important historic pub interiors that still survive here. In answering that call, *Yorkshire's Real Heritage Pubs* (now in this latest revised and fully-updated edition) aims to not just celebrate that genuine pub heritage but to share an understanding of its importance and, crucially, to sound a call-to-arms for its better recognition and protection.

left: **The White Horse ('Nellie's'), Beverley**

5

Pioneering Initiatives: CAMRA and Pub Heritage

The Campaign for Real Ale was founded in the early 1970s to save Britain's traditional beers but it was also clear that forces similar to those which were endangering our beer heritage were also ruining our traditional pubs. Marketing-led branding, gimmickry, and a 'change-for-change's-sake' obsession were all the rage and the 1970s were seeing a huge increase in the opening-up of pub interiors and the removal of fine fittings, many of which had stood the test of time for the best part of a century. Moreover, such official safeguards as existed – through statutory listing and the licensing and town planning systems – seemed largely indifferent to valuable pub interiors or were weakly applied.

Defending traditional pubs and preserving historic pub interiors were set to become very key issues for CAMRA and it was here in Yorkshire, in Leeds and particularly in York, that some of the insights and initiatives that would inspire later national efforts were first pioneered.

Yorkshire to the fore

In York, the local branch of CAMRA (spearheaded by activists connected with York University's Institute of Advanced Architectural Studies and the York Archaeological Trust) broke new ground in 1978 by forming a specialist group to look at pub preservation issues – the first in the country. It was especially fitting, perhaps, that this should happen in York since the old city, by its very nature, provided the classic material that would prompt CAMRA's focus on *interiors* as the real priorities for pub preservation. For, as the York group was quick to recognise, many of the pubs masquerading as 'historic' to York's tourist visitors were little more than pretty, well-preserved external facades to gutted, modernised interiors: this in a city otherwise renowned for its enlightened care of old buildings! What's more, as the group's surveys soon revealed, 'the genuine article' – a pub interior of real historic rarity and worth – was now just as likely to be found in an unassuming back-street local, or an unsung refurbishment of the 1930s, as in anything from the ancient ingle-nooky world beloved of tourism hype.

CAMRA soon followed nationally by setting up a specialist Pub Preservation Group with a country-wide remit, but Yorkshire

A MANIFESTO FOR
PUB PRESERVATION

Leaflet published 1992.

provided the stage for its two most influential public events of the
early 1980s – a national exhibition (in conjunction with SAVE
Britain's Heritage) in Bradford, and the UK's very first national
pub preservation conference, held in York.

The York group itself, meanwhile, was busy formulating
CAMRA's original *Manifesto for Pub Preservation,* later adopted
nationally and designed to put a well-informed and credible public
message across to the decision-makers – the planners and licensing
magistrates as well as the pub owners and operators themselves.
In Leeds, like-minded elements in the West Yorkshire branch of
the Victorian Society, inspired partly by CAMRA's early work, were
undertaking a full survey of Leeds' pubs (published in their 1985
members' journal) which would highlight the more architecturally
interesting among them. Then, in 1987, the York Group launched its
own carefully-constructed listing of York's most important historic
pub interiors. (It received wide local publicity and was published
in York Civic Trust's 1987 Annual Report). This was the very first
listing of its kind in the country and the approach taken, and the
criteria developed, sowed the seeds for the CAMRA national
and regional inventories that would come later.

CAMRA's inventories: the general background

By the late 1980s, CAMRA at national level had become all too
aware of the lack of any shared vision or understanding – between
the different pub owners and the different regulatory bodies –
about the true state of the country's surviving pub heritage and
which pubs most merited protection. Certain companies, it is true,
were taking admirable steps to identify pubs within their own
tied estates for special safeguarding – Joshua Tetley being a prime
example in Yorkshire with their 'Heritage Inns' badging scheme
– but such cases were rare. Overall there was simply no guiding
philosophy across the industry or public statement of any kind
about what our national pub preservation priorities should be.

Booklet published 2003.

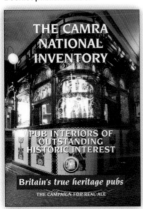

THE CAMRA
NATIONAL
INVENTORY

PUB INTERIORS OF
OUTSTANDING
HISTORIC INTEREST

Britain's true heritage pubs
THE CAMPAIGN FOR REAL ALE

The 1989 Beer Orders brought the whole crisis into urgent
focus for CAMRA. These followed a major Monopolies Commission
review of the brewing industry and presaged a massive upheaval in
the ownership of pubs. The Orders required the brewers to reduce
their tied estates to a maximum of 2,000 pubs and to sell-off any
in excess of that number, the effect of which was to unleash a
whole new, untried breed of non-brewing pub owning companies.
This was the spur for CAMRA to start compiling its own
emergency listing of the country's most precious pub interiors,
to try to make sure there would be no excuses for ignorance
among the new players about which they are. This is how
CAMRA's National Inventory began.

The National Inventory of Historic Pub Interiors

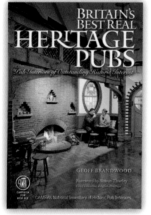

Book published 2013.

The task CAMRA set itself was to identify the most intact and outstanding interiors remaining among the country's 60,000 or so pubs. Nothing like this had been attempted before. The main aim was to list those interiors which remained very much as they were before the Second World War. It was thought the total might be around 500 but it soon became clear that it would be nothing of the sort. After six years work, the first National Inventory listing was published in CAMRA's 1997 *Good Beer Guide*. There were just 179 entries. Such had been the scale of post-war change.

The project itself, meanwhile, had been an important springboard for close consultation with key statutory and amenity bodies. It had won the support of the main national amenity societies (the Victorian Society, the Twentieth Century Society etc) and had attracted close interest from English Heritage, the Government agency for the historic environment in England (who produced a welcome breakthrough of their own in 1994 with new statutory listing guidelines for pubs). It put CAMRA firmly on the map as a serious and knowledgeable conservation body.

The National Inventory was always envisaged as an organic document to be kept under continuing review and updated in the light of new discoveries, feedback received, and CAMRA's own researches and growing expertise. Twenty five years after its inception, it has been progressively refined but its core focus – on the **internal fabric** of pubs and what is **authentically old** inside them – remains unshakeably the same.

Regional inventories of historic pub interiors

The National Inventory was a first step towards a proper structured statement of national pub preservation priorities, and CAMRA's next step was to develop a second tier of inventories, each covering a particular region (logically based, for purposes of consultation with administrative bodies, on the recognised Government economic regions of that time). Whereas entries to the National Inventory are directly, and very formally, controlled by CAMRA's national Pub Heritage Group, compilation of the regional listings is a little more flexible, with trusted editors drawing upon a range of informed sources (including the region's local planning authorities who are all invited to contribute as part of a consultation process).

The selection criteria for CAMRA's inventories are explained in more detail in Appendix B to this guide. More background information, including illustrated details of all current National Inventory pubs, can be found on CAMRA's Pub Heritage website: www.heritagepubs.org.uk

CAMRA's first regional inventory to be produced in guidebook form was for Greater London, published in 2004. It listed 133 pubs. East Anglia came out the following year, listing 89 pubs, the North East in 2006 with 46, Scotland in 2008 with 115, and Wales in 2010 with 100. There is a commitment to extend coverage to the entire UK as soon as possible.

The Yorkshire Regional Inventory of Historic Pub Interiors
(and *Yorkshire's Real Heritage Pubs*)

Yorkshire's Real Heritage Pubs is the published outcome of CAMRA's (continuing) work on the Yorkshire Regional Inventory. The research behind it has been going on in parts of the region since the early 1990s and before, including in Bradford, Calderdale, Hull and Leeds where the task of identifying National Inventory candidates had sparked an enthusiasm for more detailed local surveys. In York too, the local CAMRA group was well ahead of the game when it published *Historic Pubs in and around York* (subsequently printing over 14,000 copies in successive editions between 1995 and 2006) and some initial moves had been made towards a listing for the whole of North Yorkshire. Such groundwork fed naturally into the much bigger regional project, for which feelers were first put out and initial drafts produced in the mid-1990s, a time when CAMRA ran a region-wide Yorkshire Pubs Group. That Group no longer operates but it is stalwarts from it – Alan Canvess and Allan Sykes from Hull, Geoff Henman from York, Peter Robinson from Halifax and John Thornton from Leeds – who formed the continuing core of the Regional Inventory's compilation team, headed by Dave Gamston of CAMRA's national Pub Heritage Group (this present guide's editor).

The area covered

In line with CAMRA's other regional inventories, Yorkshire's covers the whole of the former Government economic region of 'Yorkshire & The Humber'. It therefore includes two local authority districts south of the River Humber – North Lincolnshire and North East Lincolnshire – and is why *Yorkshire's Real Heritage Pubs* takes in these areas, which are not, nor ever have been, part of Yorkshire.

However, our guide provides an extra bonus by also including two districts south of the River Tees which were outside the old Government region but are historically part of Yorkshire – Middlesbrough and Redcar & Cleveland. (The two entries we have for them also appear in CAMRA's published *North East Regional Inventory* guide).

Wide consultation

Consultation with local planning authorities is normal for all CAMRA's regional inventories, but for Yorkshire it deliberately went much further in its scope and ambition. In addition to the region's 25 planning

First Edition, published 2011

authorities, it encompassed a whole variety of other organisations and professionals with an interest in the built environment or the pub industry. (See Appendix D for a full list of the consultees).

Launched in December 2007, the consultation ran for more than a year and required much patient, persistent follow-up. Yet, in the end, it can truly be said that almost all the organisations consulted were prepared to 'sign up' their support for the inventory's aims and give what endorsement they could to the draft listings. There were no outrightly negative or hostile responses whatsoever, nor criticism of the merits of any of our proposed entries. Moreover, some good suggestions were received on further pubs worthy of investigation. On the other hand, the degrees of interest and commitment shown by consultees varied greatly, and two of the planning authorities failed to provide a response of any kind at the time. Even so, the consultation encouraged us in the view that our listings, when finally made public through *Yorkshire's Real Heritage Pubs*, had wide backing in the region: and, at the very least, that we had done our best to engage opinions and set down a clear marker.

The Yorkshire consultation also produced some important tangible spin-offs. It paved the way for a string of new statutory listings of National Inventory pubs, prompted the admission of proposed inventory pubs on to some planning 'local lists', and moved pub preservation higher up the agendas of some of the region's leading civic societies.

The entries

The Yorkshire Regional Inventory, as listed in this Revised Edition of our guide, has a total of 119 entries. The main entries – the pub interiors of special interest, which comply closest with CAMRA's regional inventory guidelines (see Appendix B) – are 89 in number. They include the region's 28 National Inventory pubs, whose status is clearly identified (with 'star' symbol ★). The remaining 30 entries – interiors of *some* regional interest – tick fewer boxes, but have merits that are of more than purely local interest and some of them preserve particularly interesting fragments. To leave them out would seem an injustice. Any classification of this kind is bound to throw up marginal cases and, if the inventory errs on the side of 'inclusivity', the fragile nature of the pub heritage overall seems ample justification for this. Even so, following careful re-appraisal, certain of the most marginal entries that appeared in our First Edition have now been dropped from the listings.

As part of the information provided for each entry we identify the local authority responsible for planning and listed building control, and usually licensing and building control too, any of which can have a strong bearing on changes to the pub. We also note whether the pub is situated in one of the council's own designated conservation areas which, whilst not bringing any extra legal protection as such to the pub's interior, ought to be a context for extra vigilance over all the heritage assets the area contains.

Are there any other pubs to include?

We hope to have identified all the pub interiors that are worthy of a place on the Yorkshire Regional Inventory. However, if there are any we have overlooked the compilers are eager to hear about them. Comment and feedback on this or any other aspects of the listings are most welcome, to:

Pub Heritage Group,
CAMRA, 230 Hatfield Road,
St Albans, AL1 4LW
or email
yorkshire.pubheritage@
camra.org.uk

What Shaped Yorkshire's Pubs

The separate introductions to our county sections (see pages 25, 39, 58, 68) give a closer account of the pub heritage and the history behind it in those four different parts of the Yorkshire region. Here we look at the wider picture, recognising that what has most shaped Yorkshire's pubs has been part of a common national experience.

Yorkshire covers a large swathe of northern England and its wide geographical diversity is reflected in the variety of its public houses. Old country pubs, scattered among attractive villages and usually built of traditional local materials, look very different from the Victorian and later pubs that were purpose-built for the great towns and cities. But these outward differences, from place to place and pub to pub, conceal a similar underlying story and one which is repeated throughout the whole country. For in Yorkshire, just as elsewhere, it has been the commercial activities of brewing companies and the way their ambitions interplayed with official regulation, mainly by licensing magistrates, that has done more than anything else to shape the development of the English pub.

Rural-urban contrast: (*left*) moorland vernacular at the Moorcock, Langdale End and (*right*) urban purpose-design at the New Beehive, Bradford.

11

The national themes

The main story was rooted in the Victorian brewers' drive to acquire and 'tie' outlets for their products, faced by an equal determination on the part of magistrates (backed by strengthening legislation) to reduce the numbers of licensed premises and improve the standard of those remaining. The one fuelled the other. The pressures which drove the brewers to acquire pubs also drove them to rebuild and improve them and this, together with rising economic prosperity, led to a massive wave of pub improvement and new building activity from around 1890. So much so that little survives to show us what the internal arrangements of pubs were like before the last decade of the 19th century.

The story of the brewers as the main acquirers, builders and improvers of the nation's public houses had another major dimension too – one rooted in their very competitiveness. By 1914, 95 percent of England's pubs were brewery-owned but the survival of the fittest in the scramble for outlets had meant an early demise for many smaller, local breweries and an ever-growing concentration of pub ownership in the hands of fewer and fewer companies. The die was cast very early on for the steady progression of brewery takeovers and mergers that would continue for more than a century. Not only this, but with the arrival on the scene of professional architects specialising in pub design, with factory-made building components widely available, and with magistrates throughout the country insisting on much the same standards, it is not surprising how much consistency and standardisation would start to show right across the national pub stock.

Victorians, Edwardians and the Golden Age

The years around 1900 were a high point of public house building and design throughout Britain. More than half the entries in this guide (65 of them) are included for the internal fabric or layout they preserve from late Victorian or Edwardian times.

Alexandra, Hull.

The pub, as we now think of it, was mainly a Victorian development. The growing adoption of the hand-pumped beer engine and counter-service in the early 19th century had heralded a transition from what was little more than a 'house' to what became essentially a form of 'shop', although elements of both continued to appear in the different plan-forms that developed. And as it evolved, the planning of pubs took on some of the complexities of Victorian society itself, producing compartmented interiors with different grades of room to reflect the subtle social distinctions that existed, even among working people. Moreover, when the drive to 'reform' public houses picked up pace in the later 19th century (influenced by the Temperance movement) one advantage of the multi-room principle was its potential to offer a choice of 'better' rooms and attract a respectable clientele. The pubs that were to emerge from the turn-of-century building boom would tend to reinforce the tradition of the Victorian multi-roomer.

White Hart, Hull.

Grand designs – and brewery tenancies

This was the 'golden age' of pub building, famous for producing grand ornate 'palace' pubs in London and some of the biggest cities but also spawning hosts of lesser variants elsewhere – all of them taking advantage of mass-produced decorative components which could add adornment to even the most modest pub rebuilding scheme. Yorkshire has no shortage of examples from this period but a question that might be asked is why the brewers here, especially those operating in the economic powerhouse of the West Riding, never actually produced grand Victorian and Edwardian pubs in the numbers or on the scale of the bigger cities elsewhere. (The Adelphi in Leeds is the nearest Yorkshire has to a large brewery-built 'palace' pub.) One answer may lie in the fact that the Yorkshire brewers preferred to run their pubs as tenancies whereas in other conurbations, like Birmingham and Liverpool, up to 80 percent of tied outlets were directly managed. A reluctance to lavish huge sums on buildings run by tenants would seem hardly surprising. An extra factor affecting Leeds, Yorkshire's biggest city and perhaps the likeliest place for grand projects, might be that Joshua Tetley & Son, its dominant brewery by far, were very late in assembling a tied estate and their finances were fully stretched on acquisitions rather than building projects at the very time of the development boom.

A further reason for the Yorkshire brewers' lesser appetite for 'palace' pubs could even be that fashions were slower to catch on here and, already by 1902, the pub building bubble had burst in London, bringing financial ruin to many investors and serving as a salutory warning. Confidence never collapsed in the same way in Yorkshire, and building continued right up to the First World War (creating some notable Edwardian interiors that are included in our listings) but the extremes of late Victorian extravagance were a largely missing chapter for the brewers here.

Other contributors

Despite owning the majority of pubs, however, the brewers did not have the stage to themselves and some of the most sumptuous public houses in the country were in fact created by private entrepreneurs or publicans rather than brewers (albeit often with borrowed brewery money). This was certainly the case with the London boom, and similar enterprises in Yorkshire were behind a few of the most impressive pubs listed in this guide, including the most ornate of all, the Garden Gate in Leeds.

In complete contrast, and at the very opposite end of the spectrum, the few simple 'time warp' pubs that survive also tend to be establishments that remained outside the clutches of the brewers, usually in quieter, rural locations. Now almost a vanished breed, their survival (in common with others among the region's most old-fashioned pubs) has been largely thanks to their staying in private hands over many years, often through generations of the same family.

Garden Gate, Leeds.

13

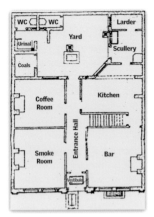

The architects' plan for the rebuilding of the Minster Inn, York (approved 1903) closely followed the 'house' layout tradition.

Plan forms and drinking lobbies

The Yorkshire brewers' preference for tenancies goes a long way to explaining why so many pubs in Yorkshire's main urban areas were domestic in scale and layout, even where they had shop-style fronts added. A good number listed in this guide are described as having 'house' or 'corridor' layouts, with internal planning that consists of a central through corridor and rooms (usually two) on either side – a traditional domestic arrangement. Some had developed quite literally in what were originally dwelling-houses, but the same basic format also found its way into numbers of late Victorian and Edwardian newbuild designs. What also entered some of those designs, and would develop into something quite distinctive of Yorkshire and Lancashire pubs, was a widening-out of part of the corridor to form a lobby for stand-up drinking. In Yorkshire, such 'drinking lobbies' are most closely associated with the western parts of the old West Riding, appearing in new designs for some Calderdale pubs as early as the 1880s but, only a decade or so later, floor-plans with modest corridor-lobbies (equipped with sashed service hatches) had cropped up as far east as York.

The Inter-War period

The years 1919–1939 are best known for the large-scale 'Improved' pubs that were built for the growing suburbs and main highways, yet something like a quarter of the entire national pub stock was also altered or renewed over the same period. A third of the entries in our guide (43) are interiors from this time.

Reducing the number of pubs and seeking improved standards in them had been a continuing mission by magistrates for half a century but 'Fewer and Better' (the slogan coined by the Birmingham magistrates of the time) took on extra significance after the First World War with a concerted drive to broaden the appeal of public houses and make them less dependent on alcohol sales alone. The ideal 'Improved' pub would provide a respectable environment with a range of rooms and facilities to encourage civilised behaviour and patronage by women and middle class customers. Where space allowed it might

'Improved' pub for the Motor Age. With its offer of non-alcoholic refreshment (advertising **two** dining rooms in its window signage) and its comforting 'Brewers' Tudor' styling, the Three Horseshoes at Boroughbridge was a classic Thirties stop-off on the old Great North Road.

A spick and span form of 'Vernacular Revival', as here at the Coach & Horses, Barnburgh (1937), was one of the architectural styles favoured by inter-war pub designers.

include gardens and bowling greens. The brewers responded with a fresh surge of pub building and renewal, mainly after the mid-1920s, and their designs for the big new establishments they built in the expanding suburbs and along major roads duly expressed the required ethos. So too did the many remodellings they carried out to their smaller existing houses, but in much lesser ways and sometimes with only a minimum done to convince the Justices to renew the licence.

Styles and layouts (and new forms of the drinking lobby)

In keeping with the drive for respectability, many of the new pubs were built in a restrained 'neo-Georgian' architectural style although a 'Tudor' style, evocative of an imagined age of Merrie England, was also prevalent – to the point of attracting its very own nickname: 'Brewers' Tudor'! Along with sanitised forms of Vernacular Revival (more prevalent in the South) these constituted what were virtually national design styles for most public houses of the inter-war period and relatively few pubs were ever created in the more adventurous 'Moderne' (Art Deco) style of the time.

Fully-equipped ballroom at the Berkeley, Scunthorpe.

The internal planning of inter-war pubs brought some new slants to the the multi-room principle. The new designs typically provided a separately accessed public bar, segregated from the 'better' rooms and well-defined as the basic (and lower priced) environment for male-dominated drinking. Some of the better rooms themselves might be designated for non-alcoholic refreshment while the bigger pubs could include large function or concert rooms or even fully-equipped ballrooms. Such facilities required careful design attention to the provision of toilets (especially ladies') and to the layout of circulation areas and service bars. An important pub function which continued from Victorian days was off-sales trade, and the provision of a dedicated 'outdoor' or 'jug & bottle' compartment was a normal feature of inter-war designs.

Interestingly, the ethos of the 'Improved' pub in Yorkshire accepted an element of stand-up drinking, and some of the region's pub designers were able to take the 'drinking lobby' into new phases of development. Some schemes made it a focal or even dominant internal space – such as at the Swan, York or, to superb effect, at the Three Pigeons, Halifax. In its most developed form (accounting for around 100 designs, hardly any of which now survive) it morphed into the 'hall-lounge', offering a heightened degree of status and comfort and, paradoxically, a modicum of seating.

'Drinking lobby' at the Three Pigeons, Halifax.

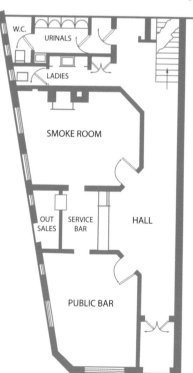

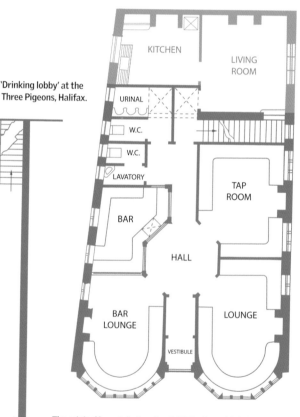

The original layout designs for *(left)* the Swan, York (approved 1936) and *(above)* the Three Pigeons, Halifax (approved 1929) both incorporated a lobby for stand-up drinking – shown 'Hall'. Both pubs have survived virtually unaltered and their lobbies, as they appear today, are pictured at *top left* and on *page 56*.

The post-war nadir

Events after the Second World War, particularly from the mid-1960s onwards, wreaked havoc on the pub heritage and brought pub design and the pub tradition to its lowest ebb. Our guide lists just 11 interiors from the post-war period (principally from its first two decades).

The pubs produced in the first two decades after the Second World War were typified, unsurprisingly for the times, by utilitarian design and the use of poor-quality materials, which contrasted strongly with their pre-war predecessors. In other respects, though, they were not so different and their layouts continued to provide a choice of rooms (albeit a much simpler one) and other customary features like off-sales departments and sometimes concert rooms. As multi-room pubs they might, indeed, be seen as part of a continuing tradition. However, such tradition would count for little in the drama that was about to unfold.

The 1960s heralded two decades and more of amazing change in which pub interiors were altered on a scale unknown since the late 19th century. There was a whole convergence of factors behind this, including a widespread appetite for things new and modern, as prosperity replaced the austerity of the early post-war years. In a buoyant economy, a series of colossal brewery mergers brought most pubs into the ownership of one or other of a 'Big Six' of national brewing conglomerates – Allied, Bass, Courage, Scottish & Newcastle, Watney and Whitbread – all of them typified by remote managements intent on wringing maximum profit from their pub 'assets'. The new bullishness came at a time when the kind of old social divisions which had been reflected in our multi-roomed pubs were fast disappearing. It was a time, too, when some magistrates and police were in favour of direct supervision – i.e. visibility – being provided to all parts of a pub from its serving area. The way was opening for the 'one roomer' and the 'visually-linked-multi-roomer' to take over as the dominant models for pub planning from the mid-1960s, enabling the brewers to operate a single (i.e. higher!) price structure throughout an entire pub. This all represented an epic break from the multi-room tradition and also spelt heritage disaster for thousands of older pubs which had their walls ripped out and their separate rooms obliterated to serve those same ends.

All of the 'Big Six', in thrall to their corporate accountants and marketing men, inflicted huge damage on the pub heritage. Bass, for one, were notorious for the vigour and ruthlessness of their pub-altering activity, publicly priding themselves on the extent of their annual spending on pub 'refurbishments'. Smaller brewers, and many private owners as well, shared the obsession for modernisation and almost the whole pub industry, it seemed, was of the same mindset.

Pubs built in the early post-war years were still being equipped with off-sales departments, most of which have subsequently gone out of use. The off-sales shown here, at the Queen Bess, Scunthorpe (built 1957), is now typically redundant but unusual for retaining its original fitments.

The older pub interiors were subject to other kinds of modern pressure too, all adding fuel to the excuses for altering them. Increased demand for food service was prompting stricter requirements from Environmental Health officers for proper preparation facilities and EHOs might also ask for the provision of indoor toilets. Fire Officers could insist on adaptations to provide safe escape routes, particularly from upstairs accommodation. More varied products – wines, spirits, soft drinks (and, much later, refrigerated cabinets to house them) – required more behind-bar space which many old back-fittings were inadequate to provide while, with the demise of table service, whole serveries and counters (especially in some inter-war designs) could be too small altogether. At the same time, certain other internal spaces were becoming redundant – off-sales departments in particular, in the face of competition from supermarkets – while changing social patterns were leading to a reduction in the use of club rooms and letting bedrooms. Moreover, improvements in central heating had made it generally much easier to do away with room divisions (rendering many original fireplaces obsolete in the process).

The aftermath

What emerged from the mid-twentieth century mayhem was a much-depleted pub heritage and also, with typical irony, a new awareness of its rarity and importance in some brewery circles. Since 1992 though, the fate of vast numbers of pubs has passed into the hands of new-style owning companies.

Industry-led preservation

Action invariably breeds reaction and, by the 1980s, certain companies were starting to regret the error of their ways or, put differently, to see a commercial potential ('unique selling point') in the very scarcity and quality of the historic pubs they still had left in their estates. Prominent among them were some of the regional subsidiaries of Allied Breweries, including Joshua Tetley & Son, their Yorkshire-based arm. Allied was notable among the 'Big Six' national brewing combines for the relative autonomy enjoyed by its subsidiaries and for an enlightened attitude to pub design and tradition among some of the in-house architects working in them. These companies launched schemes for promoting and safeguarding 'heritage' pubs within their tied estates (in London, the West Midlands, and both sides of the Pennines) which were based on proper expertise and a serious commitment to conservation. Since their selection criteria were primarily focused on genuine historic fabric, it is no accident at all that nineteen of the two dozen or so pubs badged as 'Joshua Tetley Heritage Inns' find a place on the Yorkshire Regional Inventory. Although the scheme as such terminated in 1992, when Tetley's ceased to be pub owners, the badging and display material it produced is still cherished at some of the subject pubs while the quality of Tetley's caring custodianship is still strongly evident in most of them.

That Tetley's were alone in promoting their pub heritage in so public a way is not to say that other Yorkshire companies were lacking awareness about their own historic pubs. Indeed, in Samuel Smith's of Tadcaster, the region has a rare example of a firm which retains its own architects' department and which, over the last thirty years, has demonstrated a commitment to pub conservation and restoration work of the highest quality. Our listings include thirteen of their houses.

The new patterns of ownership

Samuel Smith's also happen to be the last survivor of the old brewing firms which produced most of of the heritage pubs listed in this guide. The others have long disappeared, swallowed up in 20th century takeovers and mergers. What's more, the 'Big Six' who inherited much of those companies' legacies were themselves curtailed as owners by the Government's 1989 Beer Orders (see page 7) and huge numbers of pubs subsequently found their way into the hands of just two enormous pub-owning property companies ('pubcos') – Enterprise Inns and Punch Taverns. Nearly half the pubs listed in our guide passed to these two, whilst two dozen or more went to other pubcos, including national concerns like Admiral Taverns and Marston's. The only regional

brewer, apart from Samuel Smith's, with a present ownership interest is Thwaites of Blackburn (three pubs) but it is noteworthy that a number of our finest entries are now individually owned or run by a new generation of small, independent local breweries: viz the Garden Gate, Leeds (Leeds Brewery), the Bath Hotel, Sheffield (Thornbridge Brewery), the Cutlers Arms, Rotherham (Chantry Brewery), the Sheffield Tap, Sheffield (Pivovar Ltd/Tapped Brew Co) and the King's Arms, Heath, the Three Pigeons, Halifax and the Fox, York (all Ossett Brewery)

The remaining twenty or so entries in our listings are in private family ownership or, in a few cases, owned by bodies outside the pub and brewing industries.

King's Arms, Heath: a nationally-important interior in caring local ownership.

The Dark Side
(and a call to arms)

The losses continue

In a gloomy economic climate, with all the UK's public houses facing difficult trading conditions (and dying off at around 60 per month) is there much to suggest that our precious heritage pubs are being sheltered from the pain? Are the new custodians any more enlightened than the old and are the official watchdogs, under pressure of public sector cutbacks, sufficiently motivated and resourced to play their part?

Signs of the times!
The fortunes of the once-thriving Ring O'Bells, Bradford, spiralled downwards under pubco ownership. Its superb Victorian bar-fittings (*below*) may yet be saved thanks to the building's Grade II listing. However, with market forces and permissive planning law conspiring against its survival as a public house, they seem destined to become a stranded feature in some other kind of retail or office space.

In just the first decade of the present century, Yorkshire lost twenty more pub interiors which would have been sure-fire entries in this guide. There has been little let-up since and a full list of the principal casualties since 2000 is as follows; (Those asterisked have happened since 2007, in spite of our Consultation on the Regional Inventory and its calls for greater heritage awareness).

Demolition/physical removal: Irwin Arms, White Stag* (both Leeds); Talbot* (Halifax)

Change from pub use (with loss of internal pub fabric): Coach & Horses, Ring O'Bells*, Thornbury Hotel (all Bradford); Market House (Dewsbury); Ivy House* (Huddersfield); Albion*, City Varieties Stalls Bar*, King's Arms* (all Leeds); Westminster* (Middlesbrough); White Hart* (Oughtibridge); Northway* (Scarborough); Stumble Inn* (Sheffield); Eagle* (Skerne); Moorcock (Wainstalls); Jockey* (Wakefield)

Unsympathetic alteration: Queen* (Greetland); Grey Horse* (Horsforth); Waggon & Horses, Woolpack (both Huddersfield); Holderness New Inn (Hull); Sun (Leeds); Four Horseshoes (Milnsbridge); Golden Lion* (Settle); Commercial (Slaithwaite); Floating Light (Standedge)

Many of the casualties stem from the activities of the modern pubcos and it is perhaps thanks only to the Recession (and the dire state of the pubcos' own finances) that there has been some slowing down of investment in pub alterations. The pubcos, most of them based outside Yorkshire, are essentially property companies and the major nationals among them (who together own half the pubs in this guide) are as big and labyrinthine as the monopoly brewers they succeeded. Their responses on the Regional Inventory acknowledged its value but stopped short of any willingness to 'ring fence' their own Inventory pubs in their business planning. Even so, Punch Taverns, to their credit,

In 2005 the interior of the Market House, Dewsbury was pre-emptively trashed by its new developer-owner, just as the pub was being assessed for statutory listing. Its previous pubco owner had turned away offers that might have kept it alive as a pub, the council had failed to serve a Building Preservation Notice, and a local public outcry had come to nothing. The building itself still stands, a sad reminder of lost opportunities.

The Stumble Inn, Sheffield, with its exceptionally rare original billiard room (*below*), was being assessed for statutory listing when its whole interior was ruthlessly stripped out by a developer in 2009. Its loss exposed a woeful lack of local vigilance and asked questions about the 'transparency' now required of English Heritage in its listing procedures, which can play into the hands of unscrupulous developers.

have lately shown willing to consult with CAMRA on certain refurbishment schemes whilst it has to be said that it is far smaller players – individual 'businessman' owners – who, in league with lax planning authorities, have inflicted two of our most telling recent casualties – the landmark losses of the Eagle Inn, Skerne and the Cock & Bottle, Bradford, both National Inventory pubs of truly outstanding importance. Both these cases (see following pages 22 and 23) have served to highlight, not just the parlous state of heritage protection in their own particular backyards, but the wider concern we should all share about the 'system' generally. For serious shortcomings in official regulation, and in Planning especially, are major contributors to the overall gloom of the Dark Side too.

A disastrous loophole

Licensing is now in the hands of local authorities, with a narrower scrutiny over premises than their magistrate predecessors once had, while town planning, with a much weakened 'Use Classes Order', now allows any pub to convert to a shop, restaurant or office without needing planning permission – thereby presenting a wide-open loophole for the further haemorrhaging of the pub stock generally. This, together with the depressed price of much pub property across the country (particularly in less-favoured urban areas) and wanton disposal activity by the pubcos, has made many pubs into ready prey for property speculators and developers.

Official protection?

Statutory listing by English Heritage, and the exercise of listed building control by local councils, as well as other powers available to them through the Planning system, are this country's main vehicles for protecting the built heritage (see Appendix C). English Heritage responded very positively to our Consultation on the Yorkshire Regional Inventory with some welcome new listings of pubs and, in a more recent move at national level, they have embarked on an urgent programme of research (with input from CAMRA's Pub Heritage Group) which should result in even more. They very clearly realise that pubs are now, without doubt, the country's most threatened and 'at risk' category of historic commercial buildings. Even so, the numbers of fresh listings in any one region are unlikely to be vast and nearly half the pubs in this guide will, in all probability, continue to lack the protection of statutory listing.

21

But statutory listing of itself, of course, is no guarantee of a pub's proper preservation or even survival. The National Planning Policy Framework (NPPF), which became fully operational in 2012, has taken encouraging account of conservation concerns, reinforcing existing legislation and setting out some firm principles to guide local planning authorities. Yet the force of these provisions is only as good as the bodies charged with implementing them – and there's the rub!

Much still depends on the attitudes, interests, even prejudices of local councils and their officers and the clarity of their own policies. These people are allowed largely unfettered sway over 94 percent of the nation's listed buildings – viz those listed at Grade II (which accounts for 55 of the 60 listed pubs in this guide) – and whilst most councils might try to act with professionalism and proper conscience, 'Heritage' generally (let alone just pub heritage) may not be at the forefront of their priorities these days. Certain Yorkshire authorities employ no specialist conservation staff at all while there has to be real concern, from the evidence of the two recent landmark cases in Yorkshire (below) just how little pressure is actually on councils to abide by best practice in historic building conservation. For the prospect of intervention or sanction by a central government like the present one, obsessed as it is with de-regulation and its 'localism agenda', is remote in the extreme.

And there are further general characteristics of the Planning system which may not best serve the interests of the built heritage; its presumption in favour of 'development' and also the ease with which third party protests, including from parties genuinely seeking to champion a wider 'public interest', can be brushed aside – factors which can also tend to foster a cosy, behind-closed-doors rapport between applicant and planning authority.

The simply-furnished interior of the Eagle, Skerne, before its closure in 2004. With its complete lack of counter service (drinks coming straight from a sunken cellar off the corridor) the Eagle represented a historic form of pub planning that had otherwise disappeared forever from Yorkshire and of which only ten other examples are known to survive in England.

Below: Final Goodbye. The Eagle in 2012, on its way to becoming just another piece of housing, in a village now devoid of its pub.

The tragic case of the Eagle Inn, Skerne

Until its acquisition and closure in 2004 by a local businessman-builder, the Eagle was one of the best examples in the whole UK of a simple time-warp rural pub, hardly touched for a hundred years or more. In 2005, with unsympathetic changes looking likely, CAMRA successfully sought emergency spot-listing and the Government's decision to list such an architecturally unpretentious (but historically rare) building represented a significant shift in the national listing guidelines and made the Eagle a landmark case. What has followed since, however, has been a depressing reminder of how little stands in the way of a determined owner when backed by a lax local authority prepared to compromise on its professional conservation responsibilities. Thanks to this combination, the Eagle's conversion to a dwelling was approved by East Riding of Yorkshire Council in 2012, extinguishing another rare piece of our national cultural heritage.

In its strong protests, first by formal complaint to the Council itself, then by referral to the Local Government Ombudsman, CAMRA highlighted the Council's perverse disregard of the actual reason for the Eagle's listing (i.e. for its significance as *a pub*), their failure to properly apply conservation legislation (including the tests required under NPPF guidelines) and, not least, their failure to call on impartial professional advice in assessing the Eagle's viability as a public house (instead of unquestioningly accepting 'marketing' evidence provided by the applicant). However, the Ombudsman service declined to investigate, without offering any convincing reasons why and prompting the conclusion that, where injustices to the wider 'public interest' are concerned, they are another official body of which little can be expected.

Adding an excruciating and scarcely-believable further twist to this whole sorry saga, East Riding Council chose to give the Eagle's conversion one of their Chairman's 2014 'Built Heritage' Awards!

Another shocker: the Cock & Bottle, Bradford

In 2013, Bradford Council appalled conservationists by approving drastic alterations to the Cock & Bottle's Victorian interior, hitherto one of the finest and most intact in the whole UK.

Their decision went against all expert conservation opinion (including that of their own conservation professionals as well as English Heritage and the Victorian Society), and provided outrageous reward for an applicant who, in open contempt of the planning system, had already jumped the gun and carried out most of the alterations illegally – with no serious attempt at enforcing action by the Council.

CAMRA's Pub Heritage Group, with the loss of the Eagle at Skerne still fresh in mind, viewed this as a national outrage-too-far and one which **must not go unchallenged**. With the Secretary of State rebuffing all pleas for him to intervene, CAMRA resolved – for the first time ever in respect of an Inventory pub – to obtain top legal advice and face the risks of seeking Judicial Review. Bradford Council soon conceded that their decision had been flawed yet, astonishingly, went on to accept and approve further, almost identical applications, inviting a repeat of the whole process, and having to concede for a second time.

None of this offers any consolation for the damage done to the Cock & Bottle itself, but the case raises major points of principle. Above all, it reveals something badly wrong with a heritage protection system in which a council can fail to play by the rules, without fear of sanction from central government, and where a third party has to risk going to the High Court to seek public justice for planning misdemeanours.

Lost treasures. Prior to its recent illegal alteration, the fine Victorian interior of the Cock & Bottle, Bradford, had remained unspoilt for over 100 years, most of them under caring, responsible custodianship. It belonged to Tetley's for many years and was one of that company's first pubs to receive their elite 'Heritage' badging (in 1984) confirming their commitment to its conservation. Under subsequent ownership, it underwent a superb and much-acclaimed restoration in 2005. Some of its principal treasures came in twos: it had original counters with splendid mahogany back-fittings in *both* its main rooms, and it boasted two small snugs, both of them of outstanding quality. The front snug *(top photo)* is now no more – stripped out and opened-up – and the catalogue of other recent damage includes the removal of the counter and other Victorian fittings from the former tap room *(lower photo)*.

A call to arms

After years of careful research and an unprecedented effort to consult with all relevant parties, the Yorkshire Regional Inventory is as close as can be to a definitive, widely-agreed list of Yorkshire's most important historic pubs. Yet there are still deaf ears out there, including among official bodies who should know better. So CAMRA's bold decision to take its first-ever case to Judicial Review might serve as a fresh marker, sending out a strong message to planning authorities and others that our pub heritage is to be taken extremely seriously – and that CAMRA may not now hesitate in calling them fully to account.

The Inventory project has also discovered much goodwill out there too, and more of this goodwill, as well as extra efforts of vigilance and persuasion, will be needed if our Inventory interiors are to weather the current harsh economic times. Owners need to view them as rare assets to be prized – a unique selling point rather than a drawback – and we would urge them to take the best professional advice for any building or alteration work they propose. (CAMRA's Pub Heritage Group itself always welcomes being asked for constructive advice.)

The plea to public bodies, especially planning authorities, is to not use financial cutbacks as an excuse for reduced scrutiny over what, after all, are tiny numbers of Inventory pubs; also that they might find ways, through local listing or other means to champion their merits. Local civic and amenity societies for their part might consider moving Pub Heritage issues higher up their agendas (as some already have) and pub users themselves can play an important role too as the 'eyes and ears' for rumours of threats. If these arise, CAMRA would be eager to know (see contact panel on page 10). But there is also a bigger plea to make. All these pubs are businesses and need custom to survive and thrive. We must USE THEM – or add to the risk of losing them!

Cause celebre. The John Bull, York, built 1937, demolished 1994, is one of the most celebrated casualties of the last two decades and something of an icon among pub preservationists. It fell victim to the business mentality of its local car-dealer owner who wanted the site as a car display lot and brazened out the protests of 3,600 petitioners, York's MP, the full city council, a customer action group, CAMRA and a whole tide of public opinion to get his wish. The pub was turned down for statutory listing but this was at a time when English Heritage were feeling their way with new listing guidelines for public houses and were genuinely unsure about appropriate criteria for inter-war cases. Yet such were the reverberations of the John Bull's demolition that English Heritage's chief executive, when addressing CAMRA's AGM in person that year, took time to express regret about the advice not to list. English Heritage have subsequently moved forward with their guidelines and welcome numbers of inter-war pubs have been brought into the fold of statutory listing. How good it would be if shameless, bloody-mindedness on the part of owners and developers was entirely a thing of the past too!

(The painting (*right*) by local artist Baz Ward was originally produced in support of the 'Save the John Bull' campaign.)

East Yorkshire & Northern Lincolnshire

The geography

Our listings for the *Yorkshire Regional Inventory* follow the boundaries of the old Government region of 'Yorkshire & The Humber' which includes a strip of Lincolnshire south of the Humber estuary.

East Yorkshire covers much, but not quite all, of the old East Riding of Yorkshire. This is rich agricultural country, fairly thinly populated, with the expansive chalk plateau of the Wolds as its centrepiece and the low farmlands of Holderness and the Vale of York stretching to east and west. Apart from Hull, its only towns of any size are Beverley, the old county seat, and the seaside resort of Bridlington, while smaller market centres like Driffield, Howden and Pocklington, or minor resorts like Hornsea, are set in wide rural hinterlands. Hull itself is suffering hard economic times and its famous fishing industry is long-gone but it remains a major port city, with a population of a quarter of a million (Yorkshire's third largest).

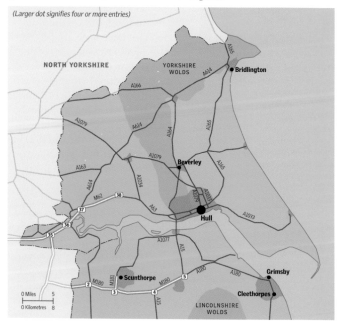

(Larger dot signifies four or more entries)

The big names from the past in Hull.
Top: The Hull Brewery Company made wide use of decorative ceramics on the outsides of its pubs, often incorporating its anchor trademark (as here at the Dairycoates Inn) *Lower photo:* Relics of Moors' and Robson's, for long the city's second major brewing and pub-owning presence, are now a rare sight. (This rescued illuminated sign is on show outside the Whalebone).

Our strip of northern Lincolnshire (the 'Humber' of official-speak) echoes much of the subdued geography of the north bank but here also are intense pockets of urban-industrial landscape: modern petrochemical plant along the Humber shore, Scunthorpe with its vast steelworks, and the mini-conurbation of Great Grimsby, still with some residue of its fishing past and the pleasures of the seaside at Cleethorpes.

Both sides of the Humber

Whether the Humber estuary is more a divide, or more a link, between its opposite banks is a matter of interpretation but, in terms of pub and brewing history, there have certainly been some notable connections. Both of Hull's main brewers of the early 20th century – the Hull Brewery Company and Moors' & Robson's – established footholds south of the Humber soon after the First World War by taking over local breweries in Brigg and Grimsby. The splendid smoke room of the Corporation Arms in Grimsby may have been a product of this cross-river influence. Conversely, it was a Grimsby brewer, Hewitt Brothers, who swallowed up Moors' & Robson's themselves in 1961 in an accelerating dog-eat-dog process which would soon put national giants Bass in control of a lot of the pub estate on both sides of the Humber. Bass were notorious for their ruthless modernising programmes and this could help explain the dearth of surviving interiors from either M&R or Hewitt's.

Darley's of Thorne were a smaller 'outside' brewer with pre-war interests on both sides of the Humber and their 1930s refurbishment of the Tiger, Beverley is almost certainly the last of their interiors to survive anywhere. Gilmour's of Sheffield too expanded their presence significantly in the post-war years as did Samuel Smith's of Tadcaster. The latter produced a number of brand new pubs during the 1950s for the expanding suburbs of Scunthorpe and Cleethorpes and two of them, the Queen Bess and the Crow's Nest, are among the very small handful of post-war houses to be given a place in our listings. Their later activities north of the Humber included some prestige acquisitions of historic pubs like the White Horse, Beverley and the Olde Blue Bell in Hull's Old Town.

The rural hinterlands

What East Yorkshire and northern Lincolnshire certainly have in common too are their low numbers of surviving pub interiors, a combined total of just nineteen. Ten of these are in the city of Hull (giving Hull the third highest concentration in Yorkshire, after York and Leeds) while the rest are a sparse scatter, with only Beverley and Scunthorpe boasting more than a single entry.

The bleak picture affecting much of rural East Yorkshire might be partly explained by the grip of the Tadcaster brewers, John Smith's and Tadcaster Tower (later Bass) on whole areas around Driffield, Market Weighton and Pocklington while the Barnsley Brewery Company, later to be merged with John Smith's, and the ubiquitous Hewitt's (later Bass), played a similar role in the rural parts south of the Humber. But the activities of breweries alone do not explain nor determine the fate of all of our pub heritage.

Owners, builders and architects

The survival, for instance, of one of Yorkshire's most renowned vernacular gems, the White Horse ('Nellie's') in Beverley, is unquestionably due to its staying in the same private family ownership over very many years. The same was also true of the Eagle at Skerne, a remarkable rural survival which featured in the First Edition of this guide. (Sad to say, the Eagle is no more, but no portrayal of the heritage pub scene in East Yorkshire would be complete without some mention of its shocking demise in 2012: see page 22.)

Several of the other gems in our listings were never the creation of brewers either. The Station Buffet (1925) at Bridlington, a rare survival of national importance, was the work of a railway company while the impressive Berkeley at Scunthorpe (1940), one of the best-preserved roadhouses in Britain, was built as a private initiative. Three of our main entries in Hull, moreover, the splendid interior of the Olde White Harte (remodelled 1881), the Windmill (built *circa* 1904), and the Olde Black Boy (remodelled 1926) were the products of entrepreneurship involving local wine and spirit merchants rather than brewers.

Generally though, Hull conforms much more to the familiar urban model of brewery-led pub ownership, improvement and new building from the later nineteenth century onwards. Two companies, Hull

One of the best-preserved roadhouses in Britain: the Berkeley, Scunthorpe.

Brewery and Moors' & Robson's, expanded aggressively and soon became dominant in the city and surrounding areas. (Hull Brewery, the larger of the two, were in fact still building pubs after the Second World War and right up to their demise in 1972). But whereas nothing of significance now remains from M&R's former tied estate, the surviving legacy from Hull Brewery includes some excellent examples of their Victorian and Edwardian work: notably their rebuilding of the Alexandra (1895), Polar Bear (also 1895) and White Hart (1904), and their remodelling of the St.John's (1904/5). Eye catching tilework was a feature of many of their pubs and their architects for the White Hart and Polar Bear, the local firm of Freeman, Son & Gaskell, incorporated magnificent ceramic-fronted bar-counters, now a national rarity, in both designs. For the Alexandra, the brewery used another firm of local architects, Smith, Brodrick & Lowther, whose practice had undertaken the prestigious refurbishment of Hull's Olde White Harte some years earlier. (The 'Brodrick' of this partnership was a nephew of the renowned Hull-born architect, Cuthbert Brodrick, designer of Leeds Town Hall and the Grand Hotel, Scarborough).

Other brewers such as Bass, Worthington and Gilmour's of Sheffield also had outlets in the Hull area, including numbers resulting from their significant takeovers of local wine and spirit companies. Yet by the mid 1970s, 80 percent of Hull's pubs were controlled by either national giant Bass or North Country Breweries (the successors to Hull Brewery) with most of the rest in the hands of Tetley's (by then part of another national conglomerate, Allied Breweries).

Beverley

Lairgate, HU17 8JG
(01482) 869040
Grade II listed
LPA: East Riding 🗘 🍺

Tiger

A very old licensed premises which was revamped in 1931 by the Hull architects Wheatley & Holdsworth for Darley's brewery (its owners through most of the 20th century). The Thirties scheme kept faith with the old front arrangement of public bar and smoke room either side of a central corridor (with service hatch). It also brought the back parlour into pub use and produced the building's striking half-timbered exterior. The plan-form has survived well and the boarded ceilings are a notable feature. The bar-fittings, though, appear to be of no great age and the second room at the rear is a fairly recent conversion.

Beverley

22 Hengate, HU17 8BL

(01482) 861973

Grade II* listed

LPA: East Riding 🄲 ⇌ 🍺

White Horse ('Nellie's') ★

Something of a Yorkshire institution, 'Nellie's' is one of the 'must-see' highlights of an old county town that itself abounds with historic interest. A vernacular gem, it has evolved into a warren of varied and distinctive rooms, still with gas lighting and warmed in winter by blazing fires in the old hearths. It takes its popular nickname from Nellie Collinson, who ruled as its redoubtable landlady from 1952

Legend in action. Nellie Collinson caught on camera, *circa* 1960.
(*Photo by kind courtesy of Pam Eldred*)

to 1975 (and whose family's tenure of the pub went back to 1892). Current owners, Samuel Smith's brewery, took over in 1976 and they have treated their precious acquisition with some respect. Their work of upgrading the pub however, particularly their introduction of a bar-servery (where Nellie had made do with a simple table and pulled beer from two handpumps against a wall!) changed the character of the 'Men's Bar' which had been its time-warp heart. Also a new – some would say, over-wide – opening was created through to the front parlour, and a sizeable modern extension built. Among many positives, though, the old semi-private kitchen was brought into regular pub use and the gloriously old-fashioned front snug, second parlour and entrance corridors from Hengate have been left largely untouched.

Glimpses of yesteryear. Corridor vista at the White Horse and (*right*) the old semi-private kitchen, which is now part of the main pub interior.

Further illustrations: back cover and page 4 (the main bar).

Beverley

37 Westwood Road, HU17 8EN
(01482) 867095
Grade II listed
LPA: East Riding 🔳 🍺

Woolpack. Tucked-away local in an attractive street-setting near the Westwood. It preserves a cosy little panelled snug with old bench seating and quarry-tiled floor – intact save for some modern-day enlargement of the serving hatch. The interior is otherwise opened-up. A pub since 1831, it was owned by the Hull Brewery Company for most of the 20th century.

Bridlington

Station Approach, Quay Road
YO15 3EP
(01262) 673709
Grade II listed
LPA: East Riding 🚉 🍺

Station Buffet ★

One of only two licensed buffets on the main UK rail network that has remained this unaltered since before the Second World War (the other being at Stalybridge, Greater Manchester). It occupies part of a two-storey block that was designed in 1922 (built 1925) by the North Eastern Railway's last serving company architect, Stephen Wilkinson, as a careful addition to the 1912 station concourse of his predecessor, William Bell. Its layout of two rooms was to cater separately for the two 'classes' of passenger and it retains all the main elements of the original room interiors. Both rooms preserve their ceilings and terrazzo flooring as well as the original bar-counters with rare marble tops and plinths. Most of the joinery is original too – windows, door-frames, the chimney breast pilasters and the lobby screen-work in the First Class room – but both rooms have lost their old fireplaces. The entire station, with the buffet, was statutorily listed in 2003 following a successful application by CAMRA and the official listing description was enhanced in 2010, again at CAMRA's instigation, to give fuller recognition to the outstanding importance of the Buffet.

View through to the First Class room, with its glazed entrance lobby beyond.

Right: The bar-servery in the First Class room.

Cleethorpes
Balmoral Road, DN35 9ND
(01472) 698867
Unlisted
LPA: North East Lincs 🍺

Crows Nest

Suburban estate house of spacious proportions and some quality, built 1957 as a pub-cum-hotel by Samuel Smith's brewery (architect, R M Bruce of Doncaster).

The three original pub rooms, planned around a central servery, all have generous fitted seating and deep-windowed bays giving good natural light. A further lounge bar was created around 1981 from the former hotel dining room (and its toilets) and a new opening, with sliding doors, was formed through to the original lounge. The outsales became a kitchen some time later.

Cleethorpes
5–7 Seaview Street, DN35 8EU
(01472) 505150
Unlisted
LPA: North East Lincs 🄲 ⇌ 🍺

Nottingham. Old three-roomed town pub by the seafront whose layout owes much to its remodelling, circa 1950, by the Sheffield brewers Gilmour's. 'The Notts' mixes some good pre-war features with 1980s refurbishment work by Tetley's. All-round fitted seating, previously stripped from the rear snug, has happily been re-instated there.

Grimsby (central)
88 Freeman Street, DN32 7AG
(01472) 354373
Grade II listed
LPA: North East Lincs ⇌ (Docks)

Corporation Arms

Once-proud Victorian town-centre pub which preserves, in its back smoke room, one of the best historic interiors in the region. This little room, which has benefitted from some recent restoration effort by its pubco owners, has superb fitted seating and wood panelling that was originally installed by the Hull furnishing firm of Frederick Eustace (whose actual fitters' labels can still be seen in situ).

Smoke room, Corporation Arms.

The pub's other rooms have been considerably altered but some remnants survive of excellent etched and frosted windows. One of the upstairs rooms was used as a music hall in the 1880s.

Hull (central/Old Town)
Trinity House Lane, HU1 2JA
(01482) 223993
Grade II listed
LPA: Hull 🔲 🍺

Kingston. Pioneering example of ornate Victorian pub design in Hull (1877: architect William Marshall) with a splendid surviving bar back-fitting that is probably the oldest in Yorkshire. The entrance doors are also of note but other old features have been progressively lost, like the bench seating from the main bar (itself once two rooms).

Hull (central/Old Town)
150 High Street, HU1 1PS
Grade II listed
LPA: Hull 🔲 🍺

Olde Black Boy ★

A rare survivor of the many pubs that lined what was once old Hull's principal thoroughfare. The premises has had many uses over the years, including tobacco dealing (traditionally symbolised by an Indian Chief – 'black boy'!) but the key interest lies in its transition from Victorian wine merchant's to public house whilst retaining much of the layout of the former. The refitting was done in 1926 for local company T Linsley & Co – the old wine merchant's office becoming the front smoke room, a serving bar installed in the rear room (which itself may have been a warehouse at one time), and the cosy upstairs rooms continuing their function for meetings. Original fittings from 1926 include the downstairs panelling (that upstairs is more recent), bar-counters and front fire surround. Designated a 'Heritage' pub by Tetley's in 1983, it was their only house in East Yorkshire to enjoy this rare acclaim. Threats of alterations in 2001 were averted following CAMRA's successful application for statutory listing.

Above: **Front smoke room at the Olde Black Boy.**

Top left: **Rear bar, previously a wine merchant's warehouse.**

Top right: **Carved detail in the smoke room.**

Hull (central/Old Town)
Market Place, HU1 1RQ
(01482) 324382
Unlisted   LPA: Hull 🔁 🍺

Front snug, Olde Blue Bell.

Hull (central/Old Town)
25 Silver Street, HU1 1JG
(01482) 326363
Grade II* listed
LPA: Hull 🔁 🍺

Fireplace in the main bar,
Olde White Harte.

Olde Blue Bell

A pub since the 1790s, the Blue Bell was a base for market carriers in its early days and retains some sense of age in its left-hand parts, with a boarded corridor and little snug that preserves its all-round fitted seating. Elsewhere there is much evidence of change, the pub having undergone refurbishments by Cameron's brewery of Hartlepool in 1965 and by its present owners, the Tadcaster brewers Samuel Smith's, in 1986. The latter involved a total refit of the plain right hand bar and an enlargement of the servery opening to the smoke room.

Olde White Harte ★

The impressive Olde White Harte has been a licensed premises since the 18th century and has parts dating back to the seventeenth. Its historic interest as a public house, however, derives from a major refurbishment of 1881 by local architects, Smith & Brodrick. Their designs for the downstairs rooms (smoke room to the left, and public bar) used various elements of the original domestic interior but incorporated them into an idealised re-creation of a 17th century 'Olde Englishe' inn, complete with massively enlarged brick fireplaces – a striking example of a 'theme pub' by the Victorians! The 1881 scheme, which also created the lovely decorative glasswork, left the old panelled upstairs rooms largely untouched. These are now reserved mainly for dining and functions but can be viewed at quiet times. One is dubbed the 'Plotting Room' – a Civil War reference to be taken with a pinch of salt, as the building post-dates that conflict. Only one of the downstairs serveries is now in regular use: both have copper counter-tops, possibly from the 1960s. The built-in telephone kiosk in the smoke room, now disused, is a noteworthy survival in itself.

The Olde White Harte's main bar in 1939.
(*Original photo by Wm.Younger & Co, kindly loaned by Barrie Pepper*)

33

Hull (central/Old Town)
109 Alfred Gelder Street, HU1 1EP
(01482) 228136
Grade II listed
LPA: Hull 🏛

White Hart ★ ⊗

Rebuilt in 1904 for the Hull Brewery Company by architects Freeman, Son & Gaskell, the White Hart was given a classy frontage to Alfred Gelder Street (itself newly opened in 1901) and fitted out in the manner of a smaller Edwardian drinking 'palace'. Its beautifully-preserved front lounge boasts a fine mahogany back-fitting with glazed-towered cupboards which is possibly unique. It also boasts a spectacular curved ceramic-fronted counter, one of only fourteen such examples now left in the whole UK and probably a product of the Burmantofts company of Leeds; another, by the same architects for the same brewery client, can also be found in Hull at the Polar Bear (see facing page). This same room also retains all its wood panelling and seating while the entrance lobby is complete with its original doors and floor tiling. Until the 1980s the pub's rear parts had separate rooms, including a back public bar with yet another curved tiled counter – all now lost to modern alteration and opening-up.

Further illustration: page 13 (front lounge servery).

Hull (Beverley Road)
449 Beverley Road, HU6 7LD
(01482) 498951
Grade II Listed
LPA: Hull 🏛 🍺

Haworth Arms. Large Brewers' Tudor 'Improved' pub of of 1925, by Hull architect Llewellyn Kitchen for Worthington & Co. Although altered, the original layout is readily apparent and some impressive features remain, including extensive panelling, the oval entrance lobby with revolving doors, the domed ceiling in the rear bar and the former smoke room (at left) where original character is most evident.

Hull (Beverley Road)
10 Queens Road, HU5 2PY
(01482) 341013
Grade II listed
LPA: Hull 🍺

St. John's

Classic street-corner local (once a haunt of poet Philip Larkin) built *circa* 1865 and remodelled 1904/5 by the Hull Brewery Company. The Edwardian layout survives intact today, with corner public bar, back lounge, side smoke room, and plain entrance corridor widening into a small lobby. So too do a number of Edwardian features, like the fine bar-fittings, bench seating, and even pipework for gas lighting in the main bar. Local protests saved the St John's from damaging alteration in the 1990s and the pub was statutorily listed in 2003 following a successful application by CAMRA.

Hull (Hessle Road)
69 Hessle Road, HU3 2AB
(01482) 327455
Grade II listed
LPA: Hull

Right: Bar back-fitting, Alexandra.

Further illustration: page 12 (exterior)

Alexandra

A lavish piece of Victorian pub design (1895) by local architects Smith, Brodrick & Lowther for the Hull Brewery Company, with a tiled frontage that is an eye-catching landmark on Hessle Road. The right-hand half (in rather stark contrast to the rest of the altered interior) remains remarkably complete and boasts a particularly splendid mahogany back-fitting, curved bar-counter and original plasterwork. There is a good tiled entrance and the main windows, some preserving their brilliant-cut and etched glass, feature gas lighting rails.

Hull (Spring Bank)
229 Spring Bank, HU3 1LR
Grade II listed
LPA: Hull

The Polar Bear's ceiling dome, a result of 1922 alterations.

Right: The magnificent ceramic bar-counter, one of only fourteen of its kind that now survive.

Polar Bear ★

The stand-out feature at the Polar Bear is its magnificent ceramic-fronted counter, one of only fourteen surviving in the whole UK and the largest of any with a curved front. Its manufacturer was probably Burmantofts of Leeds, and Hull can proudly boast of another example – at the White Hart (see opposite). The pub itself, whose name reflects its siting near Hull's one-time zoological gardens, was built in 1895 by prolific local architects Freeman, Son & Gaskell and later extended and refitted by them in 1922 (for the Hull Brewery Co.). This revamp added elements like the 'orchestra' area with its splendid domed skylight, the fitted bench seating and the striking stone signage outside. Modern alterations in the early 1980s retained the separate back smoke room (now a games room) but swept away a small partitioned-off saloon from within the large front bar. Statutorily listed in 2005 following a successful application by CAMRA.

35

Hull (Witham)
56 Witham, HU9 1BE
Grade II listed
LPA: Hull 🍺

Windmill

The rebuilding of the Windmill *circa* 1904 was an extravagant initiative by a local wine merchant cum pub entrepreneur, the eccentric William Wheatley. With its ornate frontage and other costly features, it became known as one of 'Wheatley's Follies'. The room right of the corridor is a good survival, with all-round fitted seating of high quality. Also of note are the corridor hatch and four original doors, but little of historical interest is left in the main bar area, which is an amalgamation of the original smoke room and public bar. (Opens Friday and Saturday evenings only)

Right: Fitted seating in the Windmill's smoke room.

Further illustration: page 89 (ceramic decoration)

Scunthorpe
Doncaster Road DN15 7DS
(01724) 842333
Unlisted
LPA: North Lincs 🍺

Berkeley ★

The Berkeley is a well-known local landmark on the outskirts of town which will be familiar to generations of trippers to the Lincolnshire coast. Opened in 1940, it was designed by West Midlands architects Scott & Clarke of Wednesbury for the then licensee and her councillor husband and only later came into the hands of its present owners, the Tadcaster brewers Samuel Smith's. It still preserves its original layout of three main rooms (one a dining room), spacious entrance foyer and ballroom, and such changes as have resulted from Samuel Smith's careful restoration work have been minor or cosmetic. The foyer and the public bar (the latter

Berkeley: the public bar.

Further illustrations:
pages 15 (ballroom)
and 27 (exterior)

Berkeley: the lounge bar.

separately accessed, in keeping with its era) are still largely as-built and, elsewhere in the building, the joinery, ceilings, plasterwork and windows are mostly original too. The main lounge bar retains its original counter, back-fitting and bench seating but the entrance screen-work and Art Deco-style lighting are careful re-creations of how they might have appeared in 1940, whilst the prominent fireplace, although genuinely of the Thirties, is an import from elsewhere. The décor of the ballroom, which had deteriorated badly, has been comprehensively upgraded but the off-sales area, though it survives, is now devoid of fitments and used only for storage.

Scunthorpe
Derwent Road, DN16 2PE
(01724) 840827
Unlisted
LPA: North Lincs 🍺

Illustration: page 17 (off-sales)

Queen Bess

A 1957 purpose-built 'estate' pub which appears to be remarkably intact, even down to retaining the counter and shelving in its redundant off-sales department – a very rare state of affairs. Its layout comprises public bar and lounge, accessed from either side of the central front off-sales, and spacious rear ballroom. It is possible that the only alterations here have been modernisation of the canopy lighting above the lounge servery and a replacement fireplace in that same room – making this perhaps our best-preserved 1950s-era pub.

North Yorkshire

The geography

North Yorkshire, the largest of all the English counties, straddles almost the full width of northern England, from the North Sea to within ten miles of the Lancashire coast. It is predominantly rural in character with large tracts of thinly-populated upland, including two National Parks. Apart from industrial Teesside (outside the modern administrative county) and the city of York, which lies at its heart, North Yorkshire has only Harrogate and Scarborough as major centres of population, both of which originally grew as leisure resorts. Among its scatter of smaller centres, though, are celebrated historic market towns like Richmond, Ripon, Skipton and Northallerton (the county town), the coastal tourism magnets of Whitby and Filey and the little brewing town of Tadcaster. The latter, which nestles in a low ridge of the magnesian limestone that built York Minster (and bears water that proved ideal for producing bitter beers from the 1840s onwards) still punches above its weight as one of the UK's main hubs of large-scale brewing. Stretching north- south through the heart of the county, the central plain of the Vales of York and Mowbray has been a major transportation corridor from time immemorial, and catering to a travelling public has been a strong theme in the history of North Yorkshire's pubs.

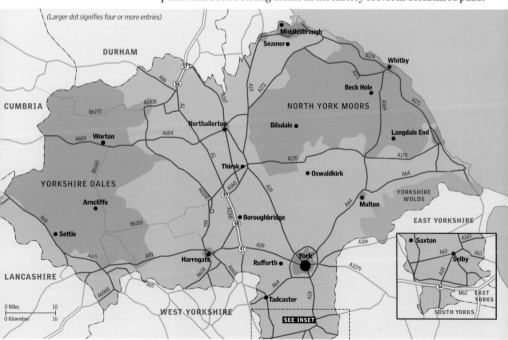

Left: Blue Bell, York.

Catering to a travelling public

None of the county's old market towns is without a Georgian coaching inn, usually dominating and lending architectural distinction to its high street or market square. Yet behind their historic facades, none of these establishments has much to show nowadays apart from a modernised interior. In York too, the city's historic importance as an administrative centre and transport hub meant it was well-provided with inns, taverns and alehouses from an early date, but its thousands of tourist visitors will find little trace of a pre-Victorian drinking past inside any of its pubs today.

Pub interiors from the later eras of transportation have fared scarcely better and we have just one rare survival on the great north-south routes to include in our listings - the Three Horseshoes, Boroughbridge (1930) a superb small 'road-house' on the old Great North Road, built by a long-gone local brewery for the inter-war boom in road travel.

East-west movements too, between the industrial West Riding and the seaside resorts, brought their own dimension to the same boom. Huge summer traffic on coast-bound roads like the A64 and A170 attracted a spate of investment in new and improved roadside pubs by companies like John Smith's of Tadcaster and the York brewers, John J Hunt and Tadcaster Tower. Yet, sadly, not one of these pubs retains its original inter-war interior and the best relic of the whole phenomenon is probably the décor installed by the Blackburn brewers Dutton's at the Royal Oak, Settle, en route to the opposite coast.

Rural North Yorkshire

Whole swathes of rural North Yorkshire are disappointingly devoid of entries in our listings, and modern tourism has undoubtedly had a hand in this. In the Yorkshire Dales, for instance, the old pubs have nearly all been modernised beyond recognition of their modest origins (usually by private owners) to cater for ever-growing numbers of visitors, and this has left a simple country inn like the Falcon, Arncliffe as a very rare survivor.

The county as a whole, in fact, has no examples left of rural 'time warps' of the very purest kind. For none of its pubs is now without a counter, or at least a hatch for counter service – an arrangement that would have been quite foreign to some of them before the Second World War. Equally, there is no denying that simple rural alehouse

Rural harmony: the Old Sun Inn, Bilsdale (on the left, now exhibited as a museum) keeps close company with its 1912 successor.

character survives wonderfully at the Birch Hall Inn, Beck Hole or in a less remote farmhouse-turned-pub like the Gardeners Arms on the fringe of Harrogate. Another Moors pub, the Moorcock at Langdale End , keeps faith with its farm 'long house' origins although the absolute doyen of this type, the Old Sun Inn at Bilsdale, is now run as a museum.

Owners, builders and architects

Where pubs like the aforementioned have survived, it is often due to their remaining in private family hands over many years, and certainly the areas of thinnest population did not tend to attract the pub-owning ambitions of the brewers. Even so, by 1900 a network of tied estates belonging to a whole variety of brewing companies had spread to most of North Yorkshire's towns and country areas. Many of these firms were soon to be swallowed up by bigger, more ambitious, competitors but all were under pressure to rebuild or improve their pubs and there were growing calls on the services of architects.

The brewers typically commissioned private, usually local, firms of architects for their pub schemes but John Smith's, who continued on the acquisition trail well into the twentieth century (becoming North Yorkshire's biggest pub-owning force by far), took the novel step in 1919 of employing their own company architect. Their appointee, Bertram Wilson, stayed in post until the 1960s and oversaw a prodigious output of designs in all the different styles of those changing times. The Golden Ball in York (1926) is almost certainly the last intact survivor of his company's great body of inter-war work but the Magnet Hotel (1934) a sizeable 'Improved' pub built for York's expanding suburbs and the Jackdaw, Tadcaster (1966), one of very few post-war houses in our listings, are reminders of John Smith's great range of work and their past presence.

York and the larger towns

The city of York itself enjoys the highest concentration of surviving pub interiors in all Yorkshire and possibly even, for its size, in the whole United Kingdom (*see city map on page 51*). Here are good examples of smaller purpose-built Victorian and Edwardian pubs like the Wellington, which dates right back to the 1850s, the Fox (1878) and the Minster Inn (1903). As for refurbishments of the same era, the Phoenix preserves key elements of its 1897 remodelling while the little Blue Bell is largely unaltered since 1903 and a true national treasure. York's main brewer-owners (and its main pub builders and improvers) in the early twentieth century were John Smith's together with the city's own two sizeable companies, Tadcaster Tower and Hunt's, while Joshua Tetley of Leeds and Samuel Smith of Tadcaster also owned numbers of tied pubs here. Some legacy from each of them remains in York's surviving heritage of pub interiors today.

Classic back-street local: the Wellington, York.

In John Smith's Golden Ball (previously mentioned) and Tetley's Swan Inn, York has two of England's best-preserved inter-war interiors, the latter being possibly the last complete survivor of the many schemes produced for Tetley's between the Wars by their favoured Leeds architects, Kitson, Parish, Ledgard & Pyman. The inter-war legacy from Tadcaster Tower Brewery includes the refurbished Black Swan and the rebuilt Masons Arms, both conceived as quality 'Tudor' showpieces for the historic city, while Hunt's reconstruction of the Royal Oak (1936) was in similar vein. The best surviving inter-war contribution from Samuel Smith's lies outside the city area itself – in their 1937 remodelling of the Tankard at Rufforth – but it is thanks to their continuing, quiet custodianship that a far older back-street pub like York's Wellington has been kept so unaltered.

Indeed, the public houses that most characterise York are typically of the 'small town' and 'back street' variety and this is largely the case with North Yorkshire's other main centres. Except for the superb back lounge of the Zetland, Middlesbrough, the nearest to a 'grand' style in the county proper is possibly Hales Bar in Harrogate. Yet the spa town of Harrogate itself, of which more might have been expected, is otherwise bereft of historic urban pub interiors: and the same, sad to say, is true of Scarborough, where the modernising pressures typical of a seaside resort seem to have worked strongly against their survival.

Arncliffe

Village Green, BD23 5QE
(01756) 770205
Grade II listed
LPA: Dales Nat Park

Falcon

Seekers after a true old-fashioned pub experience in the Dales will find a rare oasis in this lovely pub-cum-hotel, owned by the same local family for more than 140 years. The Falcon eschews modern gimmickry and the last significant changes to its pub interior, which occupies the back parts (the front two rooms being for hotel guests), all happened in the 1950s. It was then that the old back corridor was merged into the smoke room, a full-blown bar-counter created, and stillaging introduced in the servery – where beer is still served direct from a jug to this day. A conservatory extension for hikers was also added and the semi-private kitchen ceased doubling as a pub room.

Beck Hole

YO22 5LE (1m N of Goathland)
(01947) 896245
Grade II listed
LPA: NY Moors Nat Park

Birch Hall ★

A unique timewarp, lovingly preserved, comprising two simple rooms either side of a tiny village shop. The Birch Hall is an absolute gem of a pub, nestling in an idyllic valley setting which is hard to imagine having an industrial past. Yet, back in the 1860s, Beck Hole rang to the clamour of ironstone mines, furnaces, quarries and railway, and the three-storey, right-hand half of the premises was built (by the pub landlord of the time) as a shop with lodgings above for the influx of workers. The original pub was no more than a single room (essentially the 'Big Bar' of today) in the 18th century cottage to the left, and it was not until after the Second World War that a second public room, the 'Little Bar', was created from part of the Victorian shop. The present owners are dedicated to keeping the pub unaltered and to preserving its old-fashioned simplicity; indeed, when they took over in 1981 they

gladly accepted a condition of sale to do exactly this – imposed by former landlady, Mrs Schofield, whose home it had been for 53 years. (Closed Monday evenings and all day Tuesday in winter).

Right: **The Birch Hall's shop doubles-up as servery to the 'Big Bar' (via the hatchway visible at centre left).**

Below: **The 'Little Bar'.**

Bilsdale
Chop Gate, Middlesbrough TS9 7LQ
(on B1257: Grid Ref SE574936)
(01439) 798964
Unlisted
LPA: NYM Nat Park

Illustration: page 40 (exterior).

Boroughbridge
Bridge Street, YO51 9LF
(01423) 322314
Grade II listed
LPA: Harrogate

The lounge at the Three Horse Shoes is little altered from the architects' original 1929 plans (which described it as 'lounge hall').

Further illustration: page 14 (exterior).

Sun ('Spout House'). The present Sun Inn (1914) stands next to its ancient predecessor, which is a truly remarkable relic – Grade I listed, and now a 'must-see' museum for pub historians. (Open 10am–4pm, Easter to end September) The 'new' pub, though plain and simple, saw changes in the 1970s when the main room was slightly enlarged and the counter installed. It operates on a low key but flexible basis, normally open Wednesday and Sunday evenings only. (Advisable to check in advance)

Three Horse Shoes ★

This is one of the best-preserved examples in the whole UK of a smaller Thirties road-house and one whose revival has been a recent success story. Originally built to serve traffic on the old Great North Road, which then ran straight through the town, it was sold-off in 2003 by its long-time family owners and narrowly escaped conversion to a chinese restaurant. Thanks partly to its statutory listing, successfully sought by CAMRA in 2000, it has re-emerged relatively unscathed. Apart from losing original fitted seating and sustaining two enlarged openings between rooms (one now sensitively hung with double doors) its interior differs only slightly from the original 1929 plans drawn up by Knaresborough architect Sydney Blenkhorn. Its fittings, which include quality oak bar structures, oak fire surrounds and excellent stained and leaded glass, are all from the original 1930 building scheme by Hepworth & Co, a small Ripon brewery for whom this would doubtless have been a prestige project

Harrogate (central)
1–3 Crescent Road, HG1 2RS
(01423) 725570
Grade II listed
LPA: Harrogate

Hales Bar

The corner building here (with the old wooden pub-front and containing the vaults) was rebuilt *circa* 1827 on the site of one of Harrogate's earliest inns for spa visitors. The gable-fronted building adjoining was added in 1856 and the whole establishment assumed its present title in 1882, after the then landlord William Hales. The high-ceilinged main saloon bar (in the later building) still has gas lighting, some old seating and interesting bar fittings – a Victorian counter with water tap and two ancient cigar lighters as well as an imposing bar-back that features eight wooden spirit vats. Despite some evident modifications, this spacious room still has a very distinctive Victorian feel to it.
In the vaults, a refurbishment during 2013 uncovered original beams and stonework which have been left revealed.

Harrogate (Bilton)
Bilton Lane, HG1 4DH
(01423) 506051
Grade II listed
LPA: Harrogate

Gardeners Arms

In a rural valley setting at the very edge of suburban Harrogate, the Gardeners occupies a delightful little early 18th century vernacular house. Its two main pub rooms are either side of the old stone-flagged central corridor. The lounge, to the right, was possibly the publican's semi-private parlour. The tap room, to the left, with its old bench seating and ancient hearth, and divided-off only by a boarded partition wall, is likely to have been the only room in regular public use for much of the pub's history and it has a true seasoned feel. The back parts, including the bar-servery area, the games room and the curious little under-stair 'snug' are almost certainly former domestic quarters that have been incorporated in fairly recent times.

The fine old tap room at the Gardeners.

45

Langdale End

YO13 0BN (Grid Ref SE938913)
(01723) 882268
Grade II listed
LPA: NY Moors Nat Park 🍺

Right: Service to the Moorcock's original pub room is still direct from the cellar.

Below: The old wall-mounted pub sign outside.

Further illustration: page 11 (exterior)

Moorcock

Old farmhouse buildings whose front parlour was run as a simple pub by the Martindale family from 1893 to 1989. A restoration in 1992, by new owners dedicated to preserving something of its time warp character, extended the trading areas but kept all the original internal divisions. Best of all, the old cellar-servery arrangement and the pub parlour itself were left largely untouched, save for rebuilding the old fireplace and forming a serving hatch to the new 'lounge'. Closed Sunday – Wednesday evenings, plus weekday lunchtimes. (Advisable to check in advance, however)

Malton

14 Newbiggin, YO17 7JF
(01653) 690692
Grade II listed
LPA: Ryedale 📷 ⇌ 🍺

Blue Ball

In a building dating from 1714, and much-altered over the years, the Blue Ball preserves a historic core of two small front rooms and panelled passageway, where something of its antiquity can still be appreciated. The compact smoke room retains its bench seating, boarded ceiling and old corner counter. The public bar, completely wood-panelled, has a stable door/hatch to the servery. The opening in the wall between these two old rooms is the result of a 1990s refurbishment but could hopefully be redeemed at some time.

Malton

Cattle Market, YO17 7JN
(01653) 697568
Grade II listed
LPA: Ryedale ⇌ 🍺

Spotted Cow

A classic old market-side pub, facing directly on to livestock pens. The internal highlight here is the low-ceilinged tap room left of the corridor – a room of rare old-fashioned character from which even modern incursions like the flooring and fireplace scarcely detract. The corridor and the right-hand former smoke room (now accessed from the rear) also convey some sense of the old Victorian interior. In 1983 the pub became one of the first to receive Tetley's 'Heritage' badging, but alterations not long afterwards (opposed by CAMRA and York Georgian Society at the time) led to the loss of compartmentation character from the rear parts.

Middlesbrough (central)
9 Zetland Road TS1 1EH
(01642) 242155
Grade II listed
LPA: Middlesbrough ⇌

Zetland ★

The Zetland was built *circa* 1860 as a pub-cum-hotel to serve the railway station opposite, and the mosaic floor panel at the entrance and the cast iron columns on the frontage are from that time. The principal interest here, however, is the spectacular tiled and mirrored back lounge that was added at the rear in an extension of 1893. This was designed by local architect J M Bottomley for a private client and shown as 'luncheon bar' on the earliest plans. To this day it retains its superb display of round-arched mirrors with surrounding tilework in cream, browns and light blue, together with a plaster ceiling with geometric patterns and ornamented cornice and frieze. The servery is modern, however, as are the fittings in the pub's main front bar. Commonly opens Friday and Saturday evenings but opening times are complicated. (Advisable to check in advance)

Northallerton
82 High Street, DL7 8EG
(01609) 773465
Unlisted
LPA: Hambleton

Masons Arms. Intriguing little layout consisting of an old front smoke room, a lobby area leading through to a back public bar with open 'snug', and a later room (up steps) converted from a former private kitchen. Of the surviving fittings, the entrance vestibule and the original woodwork of the bar-servery (evidently once shuttered) are of particular note. Closed Tuesdays.

Oswaldkirk
Main Street, YO62 5XT
(01439) 788461
Grade II listed
LPA: Ryedale

Malt Shovel. A lovely old building with four pleasant, largely-refitted rooms leading off a dignified hallway and stair lobby. They preserve the imprint of what was once a house, later inn, of some standing (built 1610 as the manor house). Before 1939 the pub comprised just the front parts, served, as now, from the right-hand Bar. (The counter was re-positioned in 1949)

47

Rufforth

Wetherby Road, YO23 3QF
(01904) 738621
Unlisted
LPA: York

Tankard

The building is early 19th century, or older, but it is the makeover it received in 1937 – by Leeds architect H. Lane Fox for Samuel Smith's brewery – that makes the Tankard Inn special. This has left us a little two-room interior of modest dignity that has stood the test of time as a good pub design of its period. Both rooms have matching 3-light windows with colourful leaded glass in patterns typical of their time and the public bar has its original bench seating, curving bar-counter and high-quality parquet floor. The lounge's seating and counter are more recent, however, and this could be true of all the pub's panelling too.

Saxton

Main Street, LS24 9PY
(01937) 557202
Unlisted
LPA: Selby

Greyhound

Delightful old pub in a limestone village – once a farmhouse-cum-barn, and first licensed in 1871. It consists of three small rooms linked by a side corridor, all with stone-flagged floors, low ceilings and bench seating, but its actual evolution is not entirely clear. The likelihood is that the present main bar area, next to the servery, was converted from private accommodation soon after the Second World War and that a lot of its internal fitments are possibly of no great age in themselves. Until 1983, when new cellars were created, the Greyhound was locally-famous for its behind-bar stillaging.

Seamer

12 Hilton Road, TS9 5LU
(01642) 710397
Unlisted
LPA: Hambleton

King's Head. Old village premises which once combined pub and blacksmith's functions. A 1947 refit produced the fitted seating and counter in the small central public bar. Unusual off-sales passage on one side of servery, stable-door hatch (to back room) on the other. The loose tables were handmade in the 1960s by a former licensee.

Selby

4 Gowthorpe, YO8 4ET
Grade II listed
LPA: Selby

New Inn ★

A town-centre pub of long standing which was completely remodelled in 1934 and whose well-preserved front smoke room is an outstanding survival from that inter-war scheme. Sometimes dubbed 'The Vatican' (for which there are differing theories) this charming little room has fine wood panelling, stylish built-in settles, original bell-pushes and a striking bow-windowed counter screen with intact sashed serving hatches. The decorative leaded windows are striking too, with 'sporting' scenes that may reflect the enthusiasms of members of

Left and opposite top:
Smoke room at the New Inn, Selby.

the Middlebrough family, the pub's local brewer-owners of the time. Their architect for the 1934 refurbishment was John Poulson, then just 24 years of age and as yet untainted by the national scandals that would lead to his later shaming and jailing. Poulson had begun his career with the Pontefract firm of Garside & Pennington who were experienced pub designers, but this may be one of few pub commissions he undertook in his own right.

Settle
Market Place, BD24 9ED
(01729) 822561
Unlisted
LPA: Craven 🔍 ≈ 🍺

Right: **Royal Oak, Settle, rear lobby.**

Royal Oak

The Royal Oak was extensively remodelled by the Blackburn brewers Dutton's during the 1930s and given an idealised 'Olde Englishe' panelled interior, designed to appeal to the new breed of motorised tourists on their way to Morecambe or the Lakes. The lavish display (which, for economy, partly made use of plasterwork to imitate timber) can still be appreciated today, although the layout was much altered in the mid-1960s when the

former snug and smoke-room were merged and the tap room became the gents' toilet. There is still a separate dining room with more 'wood' panelling. The revolving entrance door is a noteworthy rarity.

Tadcaster
51 York Road, LS24 8AE
(01937) 834019
Unlisted
LPA: Selby 🍺

Leeds Arms. Built 1920s for John Smith's. Retains a few original features (entrances, doors) and also some remnants of a 1950s/60s revamp in the left hand room, with its canopied bar and upholstered counter-front matching the fitted seating. A more recent refit has removed some dividing walls and re-modelled the main servery.

Tadcaster
Stutton Road, LS24 9HJ
(01937) 835493
Unlisted
LPA: Selby 🍺

Jackdaw

Built 1966 by John Smith's brewery, contemporary with the housing area it serves, the Jackdaw is a good representative of its time. Unlike many of its ilk, it is not greatly altered and has quality features, like the solid oak doors in arched stone surrounds. Its design (by brewery architect Gilbert Ingham) kept a traditional separation of public bar and lounge, the latter fitted out with all-round upholstered fitted seating and outcrops of the rustic stonework that was something of a Sixties fashion statement. The gents' is still as-built, with all its tiling.

Thirsk
83 Market Place YO7 1ET
(01845) 574659
Grade II listed
LPA: Hambleton

Blacksmith's Arms. Ancient timber-framed building, stone-flagged with low-ceilinged central corridor. The historic plan-form is readily apparent but both front rooms were partly opened-up to the corridor in the 1970s and the front counter is from the 1980s. The front left lounge has an interesting old fireplace and some good bench seating.

Whitby
91 Church Street, YO22 4BH
(01947) 602906
Grade II listed
LPA: Scarborough

Black Horse
Intimate little pub of real character, right in the heart of Whitby's harbourside old town. Its old shop-style front bar has a back-fitting, dado panelling, counter-front and bench seating which could all date back to the pub's late Victorian rebuilding. A hatch to the old staircase-hall behind was probably for off-sales. The back 'Vaults', its servery, and even the striking leaded 'Black Horse Vaults' window, however, derive from an extensive 1986 refit by the Leeds brewers Tetley's – modern creations, but consciously respectful of the pub's historic importance. The Black Horse was, in fact, badged by Tetley's as one of their select group of 'Heritage Inns'.

Black Horse: the front bar.

Worton
DL8 3EU (on A684, 1½m E of Bainbridge)
(01969) 650314
Unlisted
LPA: Dales Nat Park

Victoria Arms. Like no other pub in the Dales these days and, for its basic unpretentiousness, perhaps the nearest approximation to how they once were. Equally, it has no truly historic fittings and the present layout of rooms-in-use is considerably altered. Before 1960 it had no counter, the big left-hand room was still a barn and its (three) pub rooms then included the semi-private back kitchen.

The featured pubs in York

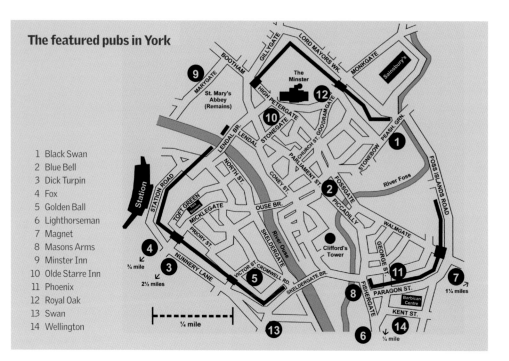

1 Black Swan
2 Blue Bell
3 Dick Turpin
4 Fox
5 Golden Ball
6 Lighthorseman
7 Magnet
8 Masons Arms
9 Minster Inn
10 Olde Starre Inn
11 Phoenix
12 Royal Oak
13 Swan
14 Wellington

York (central)
23 Peasholme Green, YO1 7PR
(01904) 679131
Grade II* listed
LPA: York

Black Swan

The Black Swan occupies a medieval timber-framed house and preserves many elements of the original domestic interior, including a seventeenth century staircase, doorways, fireplaces and decorated oak panelling. Its 1930s refurbishment by the local Tadcaster Tower brewery was conceived as a prestige project with 'historical character' very much in mind and although there is some uncertainty about the extent of later alteration by their successors, Bass, this remains a pub interior of unquestionable distinction.

York (central)

53 Fossgate, YO1 9TF

(01904) 654904

Grade II* listed

LPA: York

Blue Bell ★

The compact and intimate Blue Bell is a true national treasure and one of very few public houses to have the distinction of Grade II* listing status for the outstanding importance of its interior (the listing was upgraded in 1997). It is the result of a refurbishment in 1903 by local wine merchants, C.J.Melrose & Co – then owners of a small chain of five York pubs – and it consists of a public bar at the front, a smoke room to the rear and a side corridor modestly widened into an early version of a northern drinking lobby. Its authentic Edwardian fittings include engraved and frosted glass in the doors and windows, glazed screens with sashed service hatches to the back room and corridor, and varnished matchboarding to the walls and ceilings. The unusual little tip-up seat in the corridor lobby might be part of the 1903 works too. The Blue Bell's preservation in such an unaltered state has had much to do with its tenancy remaining in the same family throughout most of the 20th century. Since 1992, when the redoubtable Edith Pinder finally retired, it has weathered three major ownership changes but, thanks to enthusiastic and caring licensees, it continues to thrive.

Above: The corridor at the Blue Bell widens modestly into an early version of a northern drinking lobby.

Right: Back smoke room.

Further illustration: **page 38.**

York (central)
2 Cromwell Road, YO1 6DU
(01904) 652211
Grade II listed
LPA: York

Above: The public bar with its rare tiled counter-front.

Right: The bar-side 'hall' is part of the Golden Ball's unusual planning.

Golden Ball ★

This 1929 'improvement' of a small Victorian back-street local is thought to be the most complete surviving inter-war scheme by John Smith's, the Tadcaster company who became one of the UK's biggest regional brewers and pub builders. Their remodelling here raised the ceiling heights of the cramped old interior and incorporated the corner building (originally built as the publican's house in 1881) to create a more generous layout. The resulting interior is unusual in its planning, with a single main entrance, public bar to the rear, and an intimate little seated alcove beside the servery. The 1929 scheme also created the corner off-sales (now defunct) and left a distinctive ceramic signature in the glazed brick and tiled exterior and also in the public bar's rare tiled counter-front. The only substantial post-war change has been the 1990s formation of an extra room from private quarters, left of the entrance. The Golden Ball was statutorily listed in 2010 following a successful application by CAMRA and, since late 2012, its running has been enterprisingly taken over by a local community cooperative.

York (central)
6 Fishergate, YO10 4AB
(01904) 646046
Grade II listed
LPA: York

Masons Arms

The 1935 rebuilding of this pub as a set-piece in Tudor style was a prestige project for the local Tadcaster Tower Brewery by Rotherham architect, James Knight. It incorporates, as its chief glory, some genuine Gothic Revival features of the highest quality – oak panelling and a fireplace salvaged from the demolished gatehouse of York Castle – but the original design concept has been somewhat obscured by the post-war amalgamation of the lounge bar and former 'sitting room'. The separate public bar, though, keeps its original shape.

53

York (central)
24 Marygate, YO30 7BH
(01904) 624499
Unlisted
LPA: York

Further illustration: **page 14 (1903 plan).**

Minster Inn

Designed in 1903 for the Tadcaster Tower brewery by local architect Samuel Needham (a leading influence on early twentieth century pub design in York) this is a small purpose-built Edwardian pub with a layout footprint of rare intactness and good original windows, doors and tiling. Of traditional plan, it has a through hallway with two rooms either side, that at back-right being a recent conversion. Both left-side rooms retain their bench seating with bell-pushes. However, the fireplaces, most fittings in the public bar and the enlarged service opening (once a modest stable-door hatch) to the hallway are clearly much more recent. CAMRA sought statutory listing in 2009, but without success.

York (central)
40 Stonegate, YO1 8AS
(01904) 623063
Grade II listed
LPA: York

Olde Starre. A unique outstanding feature of this much-altered old inn complex is its former bar-screen, proclaiming 'Brett Bros' in decorative leaded glass. This probably dates from an 1890s refurb by the eponymous local brewer-owners and is likely to be a product of the nearby workshops of J W Knowles & Co, renowned craft glaziers.

The historic bar-screen at the Olde Starre lost its original function when the servery behind it was removed late last century.

York (central)
75 George Street, YO1 9PT
(01904) 656401
Grade II listed
LPA: York 🔋 🍺

Phoenix

The Phoenix was probably purpose-built in the 1830s but its historic internal character today derives mainly from a late 19th century refit. Its front layout of public bar (originally 'best smoke room'), side corridor with stand-up lobby, and top-glazed dividing screen all stems from 1897 designs for John Smith's brewery by their regular architects of the time, Bromet & Thorman of Tadcaster. A sensitive, low-key restoration in 1999, calling on expert historical advice brokered by CAMRA, won a national conservation award and a more recent revamp in 2009, by the pub's present family owners, was carried out with similar respect for the pub's Victorian past.

Phoenix: the front bar.

York (central)
18 Goodramgate, YO1 7LG
(01904) 628869
Grade II listed
LPA: York 🔋 🍺

Royal Oak

Compact, Tudor-style interior of three small rooms off a staggered, central corridor with hatch – the result of a 1934 reconstruction by its local brewer-owners of that time, John J Hunt & Co. (It was never, contrary to the present signage outside, a "17th Century Inn"). In a commendable move by present owners Punch Taverns in 2010, CAMRA's advice was sought and major refurbishment plans were modified to preserve most of the old Thirties fabric and layout. Especially admirable was the re-introduction of fitted seating in the front snug, replicating the originals removed by a previous licensee. A wide opening created behind the servery, however, has diminished the sense of separation of the old public bar.

55

York (central)
16 Bishopgate Street, YO23 1JH
(01904) 634968
Grade II listed
LPA: York ⇌ 🍺

Above: the central drinking lobby.
Right: The front public bar.
Further illustration: page 16 (1936 plan)

Swan ★

The Swan is a near-intact Thirties remodelling of a small Victorian street-corner pub and has one of the best-preserved interiors of its kind in the country. It was designed in 1936 for the Leeds brewers Joshua Tetley & Son by architects Kitson, Parish, Ledgard & Pyman, also of Leeds, who were responsible for much of Tetley's work between the Wars and who helped create a distinctive house-style for the company. (A beerhouse since 1861, the Swan had been acquired by Tetley's in 1899). Their design here centres on a room-sized stand-up lobby, one of the best surviving examples of its kind and reflecting a distinct West Riding influence on the part of both architect and client. Two rooms lead off (the 'better' smoke room to the rear), each served by hatch from opposite ends of the central servery. Modern touches, like the smoke room's fireplace, are few in number and, as well as the un-altered layout, it is authentic fabric like the fitted seating, bell-pushes, leaded and glazed screenwork, terrazzo flooring – even the toilet ceramics – that help make this a memorable little 1930s survival. The Swan was given Tetley's 'Heritage' badging in 1985 and statutorily listed in 2010 following a successful application by CAMRA.

York (Dringhouses)
49 Moorcroft Road, YO24 2RQ
(01904) 707382
Unlisted
LPA: York 🍺

Dick Turpin. Post-war estate pub of 'futuristic' external design, built 1965 by Cameron's brewery of Hartlepool and now one of the least altered of its kind. Its layout and many of its fittings, like the seating and bar-counters, are essentially as-built. The ceilings, however, originally sloped up into the 'feature' roofspaces above.

York (Fulford Road)
124 Fulford Road, YO10 4BE
(01904) 624818
Grade II listed
LPA: York 📷 🍺

Lighthorseman. Probably built as a pub/hotel in the 1870s, it has quality elements in its bar fittings and its window and door detailing, and keeps a sense of its old layout, although Victorian partitioning had already gone from the main front bar by the 1940s. Statutorily listed in 1994 (following CAMRA's York pilot study for English Heritage) but the original plan-form has since been further eroded.

York (Fulford Road)
47 Alma Terrace, YO10 4DL
(01904) 645642
Grade II listed
LPA: York 🍺

Further illustration: **page 41 (exterior)**

Wellington

The 'Welly' is a classic terraced back-street local (and a joy to stroll to from the city centre along the riverside New Walk). Dating from the 1850s, it is York's oldest purpose-built pub to survive so unaltered. Its layout, in the 'house' tradition, is centred on a through corridor which is stone-flagged and dog-legs past an open staircase. To the left is the public bar (with the servery) plus a private back room; to the right are two small lounges, both served from the corridor hatch and both with full fitted seating. The main signs of modernisation are the refitted servery and the plain glass windows. (Statutorily listed in 1994 following CAMRA's York pilot study for English Heritage).

York (Holgate)
168 Holgate Road, YO24 4DQ
(01904) 787722
Grade II listed   LPA: York 🍺

Fox

Purpose-built Victorian public house of 1878 which for many years was a busy local for the nearby railway works (now closed) and retains its old compartmented layout with corridor hatch. Tetley's gave it their 'Heritage' badging in 1985, then a careful restoration that same year (by their architect George Williamson), and it was statutorily listed in 1994 following CAMRA's York pilot study for English Heritage. An extensive revamp in 2014 (by new operators Ossett Brewery and owners Punch) has neatly incorporated an extra back room from a former kitchen. It has also introduced new-look décor throughout – including in the front public bar, losing some of the basic 'working' character that historically differentiated this room.

York (Osbaldwick)
57 Osbaldwick Lane, YO10 3AY
(01904) 411553
Unlisted
LPA: York 🍺

Magnet

Built in 1934 by John Smith's brewery (under their long-serving company architect, Bertram Wilson) the Magnet is one of the generation of 'Improved' houses that were designed for the inter-war suburbs. Well-preserved examples are hard to find and this is the best survivor of its type in York. Both public bar and snug retain their fitted seating and other notable features are the bar's arched back-fitting, the glazed dividing screen to the (defunct) off-sales and typical Thirties tilework in the off-sales itself and the gents' toilet.

Pub listings

South Yorkshire

The geography

South Yorkshire is the second most populous Yorkshire county with around 1.3 million people, nearly half of them in the city of Sheffield. Geographically it has much in common with West Yorkshire, its larger neighbour to the north. Pennine gritstone uplands in the west (including sections of the Peak District National Park) give way eastwards to the coal measures and the same narrow belt of magnesian limestone landscape that runs up through both counties and into North Yorkshire. South Yorkshire's boundaries push a little further east, however, to include the low lands of the Humber basin beyond Doncaster, almost an extension of the Vale of York.

Like West Yorkshire, the county's predominant character has been built on industralisation, with the main legacy here coming from coal-mining and, of course, steel making for which Sheffield and Rotherham became world famous. Doncaster grew and prospered as the location for the Great Northern Railway's engineering works and, when the coalfield expanded eastwards, the town became surrounded by numerous purpose-built pit villages in an otherwise rural landscape.

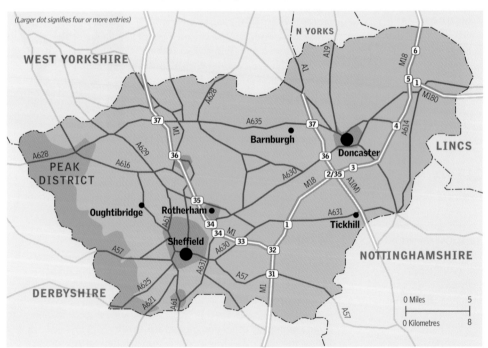

The Victorian and Edwardian legacy

The heavy sweaty industries of South Yorkshire meant big thirsts and helped ensure a ready market for the products of the area's various brewers and the development of Sheffield as a major centre of large-scale brewing. The oldest Sheffield brewery was in fact entirely rebuilt as early as 1780 by Thomas Rawson, whose name looms large in the city's history. Not only was Rawson the first commercial brewer outside the capital to brew London-style porter but he was also an early pioneer of the tied house system, leading by example and virtually forcing local rivals to follow suit. By 1899 three quarters of Sheffield's pubs were brewery owned and four companies were soon to dominate – Gilmour's, Rawson's, Stones and Tennants. At the same time native brewers elsewhere in South Yorkshire, like the Barnsley Brewery Company, Darley's of Thorne and Whitworth Son & Nephew of Wath upon Dearne, were consolidating their own, quite considerable, estates in the coalfield and beyond. Ambitious outsiders, such as John Smith's of Tadcaster also made steady acquisitions, especially in the east of the county, while Hewitt's of Grimsby were already Doncaster's biggest pub owners (after their 1881 acquisition of the Exchange Brewery there). The Burton brewer Ind Coope had a small but significant foothold in Sheffield while other Sheffield brewers, like Ward's and Hope & Anchor, remained steady players into much of the 20th century.

Perhaps as a result of their early ownership of substantial tied estates the South Yorkshire brewers had less reason to compete directly for custom and this, possibly allied with the fact that here (as elsewhere in Yorkshire) pubs were generally let to tenants, might help explain the relative absence of any truly grand late Victorian and Edwardian city houses from Sheffield. The décor and scale of Rawson's best surviving pub of this period, the Grapes, Trippett Lane is relatively restrained for its time and the same might be said of Gilmour's refurbishment of the White Lion, London Road. In fact Sheffield became most characterised by its large numbers of relatively small-scale houses, many of mid 19th-century origin but with much-altered ground floors, often with added plate glass 'shop fronts' and much use made of tiling and glazed brick (the better to

Edwardian back-fitting and tilework at the Sheffield Tap, Sheffield.

withstand the city's industrial grime).

South Yorkshire's most ornate survivor, in fact, is in Rotherham – Stones' brewery's Cutlers Arms of 1907 – although the fine interior of Sheffield railway station's former No.1 Refreshment Room, now carefully restored and re-opened as the Sheffield Tap, is of this period too (1904).

Thirties remodelling: the corridor at the Bath Hotel, Sheffield.

The inter-war period and after

Turning to the inter-war period, South Yorkshire can lay claim to another remarkable survival at the Coach & Horses, Barnburgh (1937). Built by the Wath brewers Whitworth Son & Nephew, this is an extremely rare example of an 'Improved' pub of its type with a near-intact original interior. Ind Coope's 1931 remodelling of the Bath Hotel, Sheffield and Hewitt's of the Plough, Doncaster (1934) are also very important survivals. As for the main Sheffield brewers, however, little of consequence remains of their work from the inter-war years, which makes the woeful loss in 2009 of Gilmour's Pheasant Inn (1926, later 'Stumble Inn') all the more regrettable (see page 21).

It might even be said that South Yorkshire's pub heritage has suffered more than most from the modernising carnage of the post-1960s era. Large numbers of its pubs fell into the hands of Bass and Whitbread while John Smith's strengthened their hold in the coalfield areas before themselves being taken over by Courage. Swathes of refurbishment were inflicted on a wide scale and even the local companies that survived a little longer, like Ward's and Darleys, succumbed with no less vigour to the same modernising fashions. The upshot is that South Yorkshire has only seventeen entries in our listings, most of them concentrated in Doncaster and Sheffield and with stark gaps for Barnsley and much of the coalfield.

Barnburgh

High Street, DN5 7EP
(01709) 892306
Grade II listed
LPA: Doncaster

Coach & Horses ★

The Coach & Horses is a suburban-style pub in a village setting, built in 1937 and hardly altered since. For Thirties planning to survive so completely in a pub of this type and size is quite exceptional, and makes this a true national rarity. As an 'Improved' pub of its time,

See, it works! Fully-functioning counter sash at the Coach & Horses.

Below right: **The floorplan of the Coach & Horses has hardly altered from the architects' 1936 design. (Drawing based on the original held at Doncaster Archives.)**

(Floorplan labels:) LADIES · GENTS · PUBLIC BAR · WASH HOUSE · COALS · SERVICE BAR · REAR HALL · SERVICE BAR · OUTDOOR SERVICE · HALL · REFRESHMENT ROOM · SMOKE ROOM · GENTS W.C. · LADIES W.C.

Facing page, lower:
The Coach & Horses' public bar.

Below: The 'Refreshment Room': originally for 'refreshment' of a non-alcoholic variety.

Further illustrations: page 1 (counter screen detail) and page 15 (exterior).

it was designed to look and be respectable, offering varied facilities – a commodious 'best' smoke room with bell-pushes, a 'refreshment room' (for non-alcoholic comforts), and the notably northern feature of a stand-up lobby. It was designed by Doncaster architects Wilburn & Atkinson for the brewers Whitworth, Son & Nephew (of nearby Wath upon Dearne) whose wheatsheaf logo appears on the lovely glazed counter-screens that are such a signature feature of its interior. Sashed screenwork like this is rarely found in such intact form – and it is at its most authentic in the refreshment room where the bar-counter too is original. Ceilings, doors, fitted seating and tiling are all from the 1937 scheme, as is the substantial bar back-fitting with its plain styling and multiple drawers. Even the little Andy Capp mural is from the 1970s and now worthy of remark. Statutorily listed in 2010 following a successful application by CAMRA.

I'M ONLY ERE FOR THE BEER

Doncaster (central)
154 St Sepulchre Gate DN1 3AQ
Unlisted
LPA: Doncaster ≷

Horse & Jockey. The only survivor of three public houses by local architect Norman D Masters is now much-altered but, in its upstairs meeting rooms, it retains some astonishingly intact, but rarely seen, historic pub fabric. Fully wood-panelled, these rooms and the stairs up to them preserve all of their original 1913 layout and fitments. Doncaster Civic Trust sought statutory listing in 2013, but without success.

61

Doncaster (central)
22 Market Place, DN1 1ND
(01302) 340375
Unlisted
LPA: Doncaster

Masons Arms

Included for its front public bar which retains distinctive old-fashioned character, with boarded ceiling, bench seating and a good, full-length Victorian bar-counter. The room has undergone some post-war changes, however, with the blocking of the old central doorway and the loss of an off-sales compartment from the left-hand end. The pub's back parts have been much modernised.

Masons Arms: the front bar.

Doncaster (central)
10 Market Place, DN1 1LQ
Unlisted
LPA: Doncaster

Olde Castle. Retains a number of inter-war features from plans of 1925 and 1937 and presents a striking mock-tudor facade to the old market area. It has an unusually deep and narrow layout with outside passage. Of particular note are the entrance vestibules, panelling and main bar-counter; also the glazed hotel reception kiosk to the rear.

Doncaster (central)
8 West Laith Gate, DN1 1SF
(01302) 738310
Unlisted
LPA: Doncaster

Plough ★

The 'Little Plough' is an unassuming two-roomed pub near the railway station with a well-preserved interior created under plans of 1934 (on display in the corridor). This was a remodelling by the Grimsby brewers, Hewitt Brothers Ltd, who were Doncaster's biggest pub owners for many years following their 1881 family takeover of the local Exchange Brewery. Their legacy here is a straightforward but pleasing little design of front bar, side corridor and back lounge (labelled 'music room' on the plans). Apart from the modern fireplaces in both rooms and missing side panels from the serving 'hatch' to the lounge, there is little to detract from the pub's authentic Thirties character. Leaded glasswork, wall-coverings and fittings typical of the period are much in evidence, including the fixed seating with bell-pushes in the lounge and the bar-counter with its horizontal banding. (The latter appears to have been built larger than shown on the plans). CAMRA sought statutory listing in 2009, but without success.

Plough, Doncaster: the front bar.

Doncaster (central)
Town End (off North Bridge Road),
DN5 9AG
Unlisted
LPA: Doncaster

Three Horse Shoes

Built just before the First World War by the Sheffield brewers Ward's (to 1913 designs by H L Tacon & Son, a local firm of architects & surveyors) this pub is notable for its well-preserved stained and leaded windows; also for an intact little bar parlour which, with its original fireplace and oak furnishings, is a true delight. The adjoining smoke room, though partly opened-up, has some authentic fittings too, but the spacious separate tap room has none. The screenwork around the servery would once have been fitted with sashed windows. Removal of the front off-sales has led to some re-jigging of circulation areas.

Signature window glass at the Three Horse Shoes.

Right: The intact bar parlour.

63

Doncaster (Balby)
Warmsworth Road, Balby DN4 0TR
(01302) 858214
Unlisted
LPA: Doncaster

Winning Post. Road-side house with two straightforward spacious rooms, not too much altered since 1956 when it was built by John Smith's brewery. Designed by Sir Bertram Wilson (their company architect for many years) it offers lounge and public bar, linked by a rear lobby. The old off-sales has been typically converted to a kitchen.

Oughtibridge
93 Langsett Road South, S35 0GY
(0114) 286 2221
Unlisted
LPA: Sheffield 🍺

Travellers Rest

Behind a stone frontage of decent dignity and possibly purpose-built around 1900, the Travellers Rest preserves the basics of its original layout scheme of three rooms off a central hall-cum-lobby. Especially notable are the near-intact back lounge (with good bench seating), the tiled entrance lobby, and leaded glass suggestive of an inter-war refurbishment. It was briefly owned, from 1909 to 1918, by Strout's, a small Sheffield brewery of the time, and the front window engraved with their name could be unique.

Rotherham (central)
29 Westgate, S60 1BQ
(01709) 512118
Grade II listed
LPA: Rotherham 🎦 ≈ 🍺

Cutlers Arms

Rebuilt in 1907 for the Sheffield brewer William Stones, the Cutlers was designed by architect James R Wigfull (also of Sheffield) to present an impressive façade to a newly-widened Westgate and it was equipped with well-appointed rooms radiating from a central lobby. Despite modern opening-up, the pub's original planning is easy to appreciate and the array of Art Nouveau-style stained glass is something quite special – as is the little-altered front tap room with its original back-fitting, curved counter, and elegant full-height dividing screen. Faced with the threat of demolition as part of a major redevelopment scheme, the Cutler's was statutorily listed in 2004. Periods of decline, then closure, followed before the local Chantry brewery carried out a splendid restoration and re-opened the pub in early 2014.

Above: **The little-altered front tap room at the Cutlers.**

Sheffield (central)
66–68 Victoria Street, S3 7QL
(0114) 249 5151
Grade II listed
LPA: Sheffield
🚇 (West Street) 🍺

Bath Hotel ★

The Bath Hotel stands at the sharp-angled corner of a mid-Victorian terrace and close to the eponymous (Glossop Street) Baths. Acquired by the Burton brewers Ind Coope in 1914, it was remodelled and extended next door by them in 1931 and, except for the loss of its off-sales (hence one disused outside doorway), its layout and fittings have been scarcely altered since. The lounge-snug, at the very corner, is a real delight, with simply-patterned leaded windows, curving leatherette bench seating, and hole-in-the-wall serving hatch. The larger main bar has some original fitments too while the angled corridor, with its service opening for stand-up drinking, is just as it ever was. The Bath was statutorily listed in 1999 following casework by CAMRA and a sensitive refurbishment two years later won it a prestigious national Pub Conservation Award (awarded jointly by English Heritage, the Victorian Society and CAMRA).

Bath Hotel: exterior.

Further illustration: page 60 (corridor).

Bath Hotel: the lounge-snug.

Sheffield (central)
80 Trippett Lane, S1 4EL
(0114) 249 0909
Unlisted
LPA: Sheffield 📷
🚇 (City Hall) 🍺

Grapes

This is the best surviving example of a pub built by Thomas Rawson & Co, one of the foremost names in Sheffield brewing up until the Second World War. (Note the 'TR & Co' logo in some of the window glass). It dates from *circa* 1900 and preserves the essentials of its original layout although all three individual rooms have been subject to varying degrees of modern change. The central through-hallway, however, is fairly intact and quite splendid, with its original terrazzo floor, colourful dado tiling, open staircase and old carved counter front.

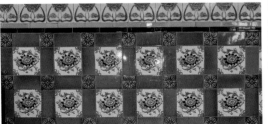

Grapes: tile detail.

65

Sheffield (central)
Platform 1b, Sheffield Railway
Station, Sheaf Street S1 2BP
(0114) 273 7558
Grade II listed
LPA: Sheffield
≠ 🖼 (Sheffield Station) 🍺

Sheffield Tap

The old First Class Refreshment Room was
originally built by the Midland Railway
(company architect, Charles Trubshaw)
as part of their 1905 station extension and
adorned inside with Minton tiled walls and
fine ornamented bar-fittings. After years of
neglect, it re-opened in 2009 following a

comprehensive
overhaul in which the
tiling, terrazzo floor,
parts of the bar-fittings
and other joinery were
beautifully restored,
while items beyond repair were carefully
replaced or replicated, including the entire
coved and sky-lighted ceiling. Certain layout
changes were made including some minor
re-configuring of the bar-counter and annexation

Railway Age splendour restored.
(*Above*) **The former First Class
Refreshment Room** and (*right*) **the
former First Class Dining Room.**

Further illustration: page 59
(bar-back detail).

of a former taxi office to give street access, while further rooms have
been added later. However, it is the addition, in early 2013, of the
former First Class Dining Room that has taken the entire project to
a whole new level. The tiled and mirrored interior of this fine room
(left largely to rot since 1976) has been splendidly restored and an
on-site brewery and viewing gallery skilfully integrated.

Sheffield (Brightside)
299 Holywell Road, S9 1BE
(0114) 243 9219
Unlisted
LPA: Sheffield
≠ (Meadowhall) 🍺

Railway

In a Victorian building that may have been the station master's house
for the defunct Brightside Station below, the Railway is interesting for
the substantial survival of (now quite rare) fittings from a 1960s-style
makeover. Both its public rooms have bright, plainish serveries with
sloped counter-fronts panelled with leatherette to match the seating.
The public bar (once two rooms) has intact fitted seating and an
above-bar lighting canopy, typical of those times. The lounge
extension is probably 1970s. Old offsales window in entrance lobby.

Sheffield (Handsworth)
400 Handsworth Road, S13 9BZ
(0114) 254 1050
Unlisted
LPA: Sheffield 🍺

Cross Keys

The Cross Keys is a three-roomed pub with lots of vintage fittings,
housed in an old vernacular building that stands virtually within the
churchyard. The back parts are the main interest here, with the snug
a particular delight. This little room, refitted probably in the 1920s
and largely untouched since, has all its original seating, panelling and
Art Deco fire surround. There is more old seating in the other rooms
and a (disused) corridor hatch near the entrance. The servery and
bar-fittings, though, are all modern.

Sheffield (Heeley)
615 London Road, S2 4HT
(0114) 255 1500
Grade II listed
LPA: Sheffield

White Lion

The White Lion is a real mixture of the old and the new (not always easy to tell apart, thanks to Tetley's respectful refurbishment work of the 1980s). It is chiefly interesting, though, for what survives of an early twentieth century remodelling by the Sheffield brewers Duncan

Gilmour & Co, who acquired it in 1900. A richly-tiled central corridor, with its original service-opening, leads between the old front bar and smoke room and past two (part-altered) glazed snugs, to a vast modernised former concert room at the rear. The pub's historic merits earned it recognition, in 1989, as one of Tetley's select group of 'Heritage Inns'.

Sheffield (Manor)
239 Manor Lane, S2 1UJ
(0114) 272 4768
Unlisted
LPA: Sheffield

Manor Castle

The Manor Castle came into the hands of the Burton brewers Ind Coope following their 1914 takeover of the local Hooson's brewery. It was given a major refit around 1930, of which the two delightful small 'lounges' are notable remnants. Both preserve their wood panelling, fixed seating and bell-pushes. The front lounge has an attractive curved bar-counter while service to the back lounge is via a glazed 'stable door'. Apart from two surviving Thirties fireplaces, the large main bar is wholly modernised.

Right: **Manor Castle**: the back lounge

Tickhill
Sunderland Street, DN11 9QJ
(01302) 742977
Unlisted
LPA: Doncaster

Scarbrough Arms

Old village inn, still with three rooms, but chiefly noteworthy for its unusual 1950s 'Barrel Room' dating from the time it belonged to the Wath brewers Whitworth, Son & Nephew. This very impressive little room (altered only by a 1980s cut-through to the tap room) has a concave-fronted oak counter, oak fixed seating, ply-panelled walls, and loose furniture made from casks – said to be the work of George Milburn, tenant-licensee from 1953 to 1958, who also worked as a blacksmith at nearby Harworth Colliery. The other rooms are of much less note, though both have fittings that might date back to the 1950s or 60s.

Right: **Scarbrough Arms**:
the 'Barrel Room'.

Pub listings   **West Yorkshire**

The geography

Yorkshire's most populous county is probably most famed for the old West Riding industries that were such a part of Britain's Industrial Revolution – not just the textile industry but also the engineering that grew alongside it and the coal-mining that fuelled it. Certainly the predominant character here is of industrialisation and urbanisation, extending from the Pennine gritstone valleys in the west with their famous old textile towns to the flatter coalfield areas in the east. The city of Leeds, now unrivalled as the modern-day regional capital, sits between them and not far north of the old county town of Wakefield. The county's western boundary embraces a stretch of the Peak District National Park while its eastern edges, fringing the Vale of York, are marked by a belt of low magnesian limestone hills.

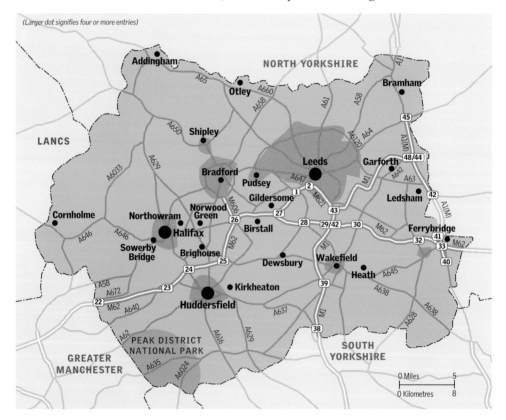

(*Larger dot signifies four or more entries*)

City style: the Garden Gate, Leeds.

Country style: the Olde White Beare, Norwood Green (entrance to snug).

Urbanisation and variety

The development of West Yorkshire's public houses went hand in hand with its Victorian and later urbanisation, and produced a variety of urban pub types to rival most other parts of the country. Only the very grandest Victorian and Edwardian drinking 'palaces' (which were largely confined to London and a few of the UK's biggest cities) were missing from the repertoire; yet in the Garden Gate, Leeds and the Cock & Bottle, Bradford, West Yorkshire was able to produce ornate pubs of a similarly high order. But the story of historic pub survival in the county's two largest cities is a contrasting one. Whereas Leeds has twelve entries in our listings, the number now left within Bradford's (pre-1974) city boundary has dwindled to just two, one of which – the aforementioned Cock & Bottle – is but a shadow of its former self, having been closed-down since 2011 and shamefully stripped of much of its priceless interior (see page 23).

Few of the very oldest pubs in the pre-industrial Pennine settlements too, or in the countryside areas that intersperse the conurbation, have been spared from modern pressures for internal alteration. Yet at the Olde White Beare, Norwood Green can be found one of the finest and rarest old snugs in all England, while the King's Arms at Heath still displays something of its cottage origins.

The owners and builders: pre-1914

In West Yorkshire, as elsewhere, the competitive drive by brewers to acquire and develop tied estates in the later 19th century led to the creation of high-quality houses in the larger centres and the smaller towns alike. Some like the Sportsman, Halifax (1904) were part of municipal street improvement schemes while the New Beehive, Bradford (1901) was a rare case of design by the city council itself. There were contrasts in the activities of the brewers too. Certain of them, such as Tetley's in Leeds. Whittaker's in Bradford and Bentley & Shaw in Huddersfield, enjoyed such renown and good profit from their products that they had less incentive to acquire property and were much later into the field. Some of the most lavish houses in Leeds, including the Adelphi (1901) and the Rising Sun (1899) were in fact produced by Tetley's city rivals, the Leeds & Wakefield (Melbourne) Breweries, using the Leeds architect Thomas Winn, while the marvellous creations of Whitelock's (1895), the Garden Gate (1902) and the Cardigan Arms (1896, also designed by Winn) were private initiatives by individual entrepreneurs or publicans. In Huddersfield the sober design of the town's pubs, together with their delayed acquisition by brewers, is in no small part due to the control exerted by the Ramsden estate who owned most of the town centre until 1920.

Memories preserved.
A mosaic tablet outside the Beech, Leeds (1937) proclaims the wares of its original builders, the long-gone Melbourne Brewery, whilst (*below*) a window there still bears their locally-famous 'bowing courtier' trademark.

Art Deco door signage at the Three Pigeons, Halifax (1932).

The inter-war period

It was in the second major wave of pub building and improving, after the First World War, that some of the brewers started to develop their own distinctive house styles, relying for the most part on favoured firms of (usually local) architects. Kitson, Parish Ledgard & Pyman of Leeds were commissioned by Joshua Tetley & Son for most of the Leeds brewer's inter-war designs and it was Kitson's who were responsible for developing the recognisable Tetley house style that can still be found across many parts of Yorkshire, and even into Lancashire, today. Huddersfield's largest brewer, Bentley & Shaw, favoured their local firm of Abbey Hanson, while Webster's of Halifax used the Halifax architects Jackson & Fox for all their work.

Another leading Halifax brewer, Ramsden's, also employed Jackson & Fox, as well as Glendinning & Hanson, to create some quality 'Tudor' designs in their home town, like the Royal Oak (1931), now 'Dirty Dick's') and the Halfway House (1932). This nationally popular style was also favoured by 'outsider' brewers, not least Stones of Sheffield and Wilsons of Manchester who had modest estates in the Huddersfield area and employed the local architect Joseph Berry (the Victoria at Newsome being a surviving example of his work). The most influential outsiders, though, were John Smith's of Tadcaster, who were responsible for large numbers of new houses and employed their own in-house design team under company architect, Bertram Wilson. Their designs were executed in a variety of styles but always with high quality internal fittings. Two Leeds pubs, the Grove and the Hanover Arms, though altered, provide examples of the company's refurbishment and newbuild work of the inter-war period. Another Tadcaster brewer, Samuel Smith's, using Leeds architect H. Lane Fox, produced the only thoroughly 'Moderne' (Art Deco) pub building that appears in our listings – the New Inn at Gildersome – but, truth to tell, little of its original interior now survives.

The main espousers of the modern movement were in fact Webster's of Halifax, Beverley's of Wakefield and Melbourne Brewery of Leeds. Both the latter employed the Pontefract architects Garside & Pennington and Art Deco touches can be observed at Melbourne's Beech in Leeds (1931) and Gaping Goose at Garforth. However, the greatest survival of Art Deco internal styling is at the Three Pigeons, Halifax (1932) designed for Webster's brewery by their regular architects, Jackson & Fox.

The overall pattern of survival

Half of our entries for West Yorkshire are for Victorian or Edwardian interiors and almost as many are for refurbishments or new build work of the inter-war period. It is a matter for regret, however, that none of the big inter-war suburban or roadside houses, which were built in numbers for the coalfield communities or the Leeds suburbs, are represented in our listings. Such has been the force of post-war alteration to their interiors. Even for interiors created in the post-war period itself, there are now few from the 1950s and early 1960s that have been able to survive intact and we have felt confident in identifying a small handful as good examples of their type – among them the Rocking Horse, Wakefield (1955) and the 1962 refurbishments of the White Horse, Sowerby Bridge and the Chequers, Ledsham.

As for the creators themselves (the old brewing companies mentioned in these pages) only Samuel Smith's of Tadcaster survived the merger mania of the mid twentieth century. Locally-famous names like Melbourne, Ramsden and William Whittaker were taken over by Tetley's, before they in turn became part of the national giant Allied Breweries and, ultimately, the global giant Carlsberg (who finally shut down their Leeds brewery in 2011). Webster's were bought out by Watney while Hammond's, briefly one of the biggest brewers in the North (having absorbed Bentley & Shaw and Tadcaster Tower on the way) disappeared into the maw of Bass, now part of the US giant Coor's. Dutton's succumbed to Whitbread and the picture of 'consolidation' was all-but complete when John Smith's, for years a major predator themselves, became a part of Courage and, latterly, of Heineken.

Addingham
136 Main Street, LS29 0NS
(01943) 830278
Grade II listed
LPA: Bradford

Crown
Old village house which has altered with the times but which preserves two simply-furnished and largely untouched old rooms in its right-hand half (either side of an original cross passage and enclosed staircase): one, the front snug, has matchboard-backed seating and a simple fireplace; the other, a larger back smoke room, has fitted seating, boarded ceiling, service hatch and an old enamel door-sign. The deep lounge area is clearly a modern amalgamation of two former rooms and the room further left is a later creation too.

Birstall
5 Kirkgate, WF17 9HE
(01274) 873039
Grade II listed
LPA: Kirklees

Black Bull. Included solely for its upstairs function room which has two elaborately carved and painted 'boxes' – most likely deriving from its former use as a lodge for the Ancient Order of Druids (who had connections here from 1834). The rest of the pub's interior was modernised around 1960 by the Blackburn brewers Dutton's.

'Box' at the Black Bull: a reminder of the important historic role public houses played as venues for the meetings and ceremonials of men's friendly societies.

71

Bradford (central)
93 Barkerend Road, BD3 9AA
Grade II listed
LPA: Bradford
≈ (Forster Square)

Cock & Bottle ⊗ Closed since 2011 and reduced to shreds of its former self by the actions of a seemingly shameless owner and lax planning authority (see page 23). The old central servery, some rare glazed screenwork and other decorative detail – though splendid in themselves – are now the token remnants of a 1901 refurbishment that made this one of the UK's very finest late-Victorian pub interiors.

Bradford (central)
169–171 Westgate, BD1 3AA
(01274) 721784
Unlisted
LPA: Bradford
≈ (Forster Square) 🍺

New Beehive ★

The New Beehive blends elements of its original late Victorian interior with a 1936 remodelling by William Whitaker & Co, one of Bradford's leading brewers of the inter-war era. It was rebuilt in 1901 as part of the municipal improvement of Westgate (replacing an old coaching inn) and the plans for its construction were drawn up by the city architect & surveyor of the time, J H Cox. The original three rooms are to a typical 'house' plan, with the central corridor elaborated into a drinking hallway. In the front public bar, the curving oak bar-counter, arcaded back-fitting and bench seating are all fittings from the 1901 scheme. The old fabric and décor elsewhere is from the 1936 refurbishment and seen at its best in the back-left smoke room and the panelled hallway lobby. The gents' toilet, the tiled corridor to it, and the back concert room (now lacking in original fittings) are also of 1936. CAMRA sought statutory listing in 2009, but without success.

Below right: **The New Beehive's public bar.**

Below: **The back smoke room.**

Further illustration: **page 11 (exterior)**

Bramham

Town Hill, LS23 6QQ
(01937) 843570
Unlisted
LPA: Leeds 🔲 🍺

Swan

Tucked away in the upper part of the village, this small, drinks-only local (dubbed 'Top House') is excellent reward for the short climb. Good, old-fashioned character prevails strongly in its intimate front parts and, even in its altered back areas, the imprint of the original through-corridor layout is still very evident. The changes at the rear, probably in the early 1960s, removed some internal walls, brought the back-right room into pub use, and relocated the servery (note the stranded 'hatch', suggesting its earlier position).

Brighouse

37 Bethel Street, HD6 1JN
Unlisted
LPA: Calderdale 🚉 🍺

Old Ship. Formerly Prince of Wales; 1925, by architects Jackson & Fox for Webster's brewery. This pub is notable for its 'Tudor' décor – oak panelling, fireplaces, ceiling, friezes – and its elaborate external wood carving by local master craftsman H P Jackson (although more is made of HMS Donegal, the source of the timber!). A thoughtful refurbishment in 2009 has brought some admirable improvements.

Cornholme

853 Burnley Road, Portsmouth,
OL14 7EW   (01706) 812796
Unlisted
LPA: Calderdale 🍺

Glen View. Very conspicuously opened-up at its heart, and its servery has clearly been re-positioned (possibly in the 1950s). It retains, however, the footprint of its former layout, its still separate 'General Room' and a number of old features – serving hatch, bell-pushes, some good fitted seating and matchboarded ceilings.

Dewsbury (central)

Halifax Road, WF13 2AL
(01924) 461095
Unlisted
LPA: Kirklees 🚉

Bath. The chief interest here is the front layout of corridor with hatch, front snug with boarded ceiling and fixed seating and, most notably, the tap room, with its fitted settles and backed by glazed screening. The origin of the unusual internal planning is unclear but the fitting-out of the servery and rear lounge is plainly of recent date.

Dewsbury (central)

Crackenedge Lane, WF13 1QY
Grade II listed
LPA: Kirklees 🔲 🚉

Central Station Hotel

Built in 1903 as a pub-hotel to serve a now-defunct railway and close to Dewsbury's renowned market. Its internal restoration is a continuing work-in-progress, making much use of architectural salvage but also preserving some good original elements. The spacious tap room retains its striking stained glass skylight, its curved bar-

counter and some old bench seating while the smaller smoke room, which shares the single storey end of the building, keeps its original curve of high quality fitted seating. A particular highlight is the glazed screenwork with original Art Nouveau decoration in the central lobby area, framing both the bar-servery and the entrance vestibule there.

Ferrybridge
The Square, WF11 8ND
(01977) 312169
Unlisted
LPA: Wakefield 🍺

Golden Lion

One-time coaching inn beside the ancient river bridge and in the shadow of the 'old' A1 flyover. Its generous rooms surround a wide hallway lobby and there are all the hallmarks of a stylish inter-war makeover. Leaded glasswork, so characteristic of Tetley's revamps between the Wars, is much in evidence and the shuttered servery is particularly noteworthy, as is the bar frontage to the back room (now a games room).

Garforth
41 Selby Road, LS25 1LR
(0113) 286 2127
Unlisted
LPA: Leeds 🍺

Gaping Goose. Revamped in 1935 by the Melbourne Brewery of Leeds (architects Pennington, Hustler & Taylor of Pontefract). Various doors and windows with Art Deco motifs survive from that scheme, along with the mosaic-tiled entrance floor and what fittings remain in the small front snug. The 'Tudor Bar', a 1950s addition, remains intact, but the pub's main interior is much altered.

Gildersome
Church Street, Gildersome,
Morley, LS27 7AE
(0113) 253 4821
Unlisted
LPA: Leeds 🍺

New Inn. Dashingly 'Moderne' (Art Deco) on the outside, and the only example of this rare building type in our listings, the New Inn is a design of 1934 by Leeds architect H Lane Fox for present owners, Samuel Smith's. The brewery have made efforts to reverse some of their own opening-up of the 1960s and 70s but the only true remains of the Thirties interior are doors and surrounds to the entrance area.

Halifax (central)
1 Clare Road, HX1 2HX
Grade II listed
LPA: Calderdale 📷 ⇌ 🍺

Dirty Dick's

This pub, formerly the 'Royal Oak', was a prestige Brewers' Tudor extravaganza, reconstructed in 1931 as the brewery tap for Ramsden's (by Halifax architects Jackson & Fox). The original four-room layout has been merged into one, probably in the 1960s, but the bar, oak panelling and three good fireplaces survive. The leaded windows are elaborately decorated with heraldic motifs and the intricate wood-carving is work by a master craftsman, H.P. Jackson of nearby Coley. Statutorily listed in 1994 following a successful application by CAMRA.

Halifax (central)
Old Cock Yard, HX1 1DS
Grade II listed
LPA: Calderdale 🄲 ≈
Illustration: page 2 (window)

Old Cock. The sole interest here is the upstairs 'Oak Room', said to have been purpose-built as a banqueting room for this truly ancient inn (dating back to the 1660s). It boasts elaborate decoration of great age and richly detailed windows of 1879 by Powell of Leeds, depicting the inn's history. It can be viewed by asking at the bar.

Halifax (central)
Crown Street, HX1 1JB
Grade II listed
LPA: Calderdale 🄲 ≈ 🍺

Sportsman

Ancient inn, remodelled in 1904 to designs by W.H.D.Horsfall, and now Halifax's only example of a substantially-surviving Edwardian interior. Four rooms with elaborate ceilings and much of their original fitted seating lead off a central drinking lobby that features an ornate staircase. The layout has been partly opened-out but the former dining room at front-right is intact, with oak-panelling and good leaded windows depicting sporting scenes. Statutorily listed in 1995 following a successful application by CAMRA.

Halifax (central)
1 Sun Fold, South Parade HX1 2LX
(01422) 347001
Grade II listed
LPA: Calderdale ≈ 🍺

The bar lounge at the Three Pigeons, with view through to the central drinking lobby.

Three Pigeons ★

A marvellous little Thirties survival which combines Art Deco internal styling with one of the best, and most interesting, examples of the northern stand-up 'drinking lobby'. Rebuilt in 1932 for Samuel Webster & Son, one of Halifax's leading brewers of that time, and designed by local architects Jackson & Fox (who undertook all of Websters' commissions between the Wars) the Three Pigeons preserves an interior that is rare and remarkable. Its layout is unusual, with the drinking lobby as a superb little centrepiece from which three rooms and the servery all radiate. The lobby itself, moreover, is the only octagonal version of its type now known to survive. There is much else to delight: flush-panelling in oak veneer, stylish metal-ribbon signage on doors, geometric patterning in the lobby's terrazzo floor and stepped plasterwork to its 'dome' (echoing the room cornices). Also noteworthy are the timber fire surrounds, fitted seating throughout, and a good bar back-fitting with mirrored panels, one featuring a vintage advertisement for 'Green Label' beer. A sensitive restoration in 2006 won a prestigious national conservation award for current owners Ossett Brewery, and the pub was statutorily listed in 2010, following a successful application by CAMRA. Both the 2006 scheme and a further sympathetic refurbishment carried out in early 2014 have successfully created extra pub rooms (from former private accommodation at the rear) without compromising the pub's essential historic core.

Art Deco door signage.

Further illustrations: page 16 (central drinking lobby: 1929 plan) and page 70 (door signage)

Halifax (King Cross)
10 Horsfall Street, HX1 3HG
(01422) 350169
Unlisted
LPA: Calderdale

Big Six

Local of rare character, with an unmade road on its garden side and set within a row of terraced houses. Erected in 1857 as a purpose-built beer house with its own brewhouse, it has an unusual layout and retains many of its internal fittings. These include oak-framed fitted seating,

wood-panelling and a fine bar back-fitting, all probably dating from soon after its acquisition by local brewers Ramsden's in 1928. The layout consists of a central corridor with two partly opened-up rooms plus a bar-lounge and an excellent, cosy snug. (The games room is very recent). Tetley's gave the Big Six their 'Heritage' badging in the mid-1980s and the refurbishment work from around that time bears their distinctive signature.

Halifax (Pellon)
39 Moor End Road, HX2 0HF
(01422) 361215
Unlisted
LPA: Calderdale

Halfway House

A large, 'Improved' house built 1932 for Ramsden's brewery by local architects Glendinning & Hanson and designed with a central hall-lounge – an advance on the old-style drinking lobby, equipped with some seating and containing the main servery. Impressive counter and bar-back (but with typical modern pot-shelf). Other original features are the unused off-sales, some of the seating and the lofty vaulted function room upstairs. The former separate snug and smoke room were merged into one end of the hall-lounge during the 1970s.

Halifax (Pellon)
38 Sutcliffe Street, HX2 0HG
Unlisted
LPA: Calderdale

New Street

This is a classic end-of-terrace local, a former beerhouse, which was remodelled by Webster's brewery in 1935 (architects, Jackson & Fox). Their revamp included features, like the stand-up lobby, that were being designed into their much larger new pubs of the time – and the New Street preserves the planning and many of the fittings from the inter-war scheme. It has a tiny front bar, rear lounge, tap room and a dog-legging central corridor opening into a small central stand-up lobby. Original fittings include good oak-panelled doors and seating with Art Deco stepped armrests. (The fireplaces and lounge counter are later). CAMRA sought statutory listing in 2009, without success.

Heath

Heath Common, WF1 5SL
(01924) 377527
Grade II listed
LPA: Wakefield 🇨 🍺

King's Arms, Heath: front snug.

Further illustration: **page 19** (corridor).

King's Arms ★

Almost a textbook example of how a pub can undergo enormous
enlargement without too seriously compromising its historic core.
The old core here is the time-worn, wood-panelled arrangement of
front bar, corridor entrance, and front snug which originated from
cottages during the 1840s and formed the entire extent of the public
house up until the Second World War. It still functions as the 'pub'
heart of a pub-restaurant that has expanded into adjoining former
stabling, barn and domestic accommodation and spawned a large
conservatory at the rear. The lounge to the right, although a post-war
conversion, has some attractive adornments of its own – fireplaces made
of salvaged materials from Heath Old Hall and a carved coat of arms
of 1980s vintage. The King's Arms has over thirty working gaslights –
most of them modern, but possibly the largest number in any UK pub.

Huddersfield (central)

Victoria Lane, HD1 2QF
(01484) 950585
Unlisted
LPA: Kirklees 🇨 ⇌ 🍺

Albert

Built 1879, the Albert was purpose-designed by Edward Hughes, a
leading contributor to Huddersfield's central Victorian architecture.
It retains good old-fashioned character
and its impressive marble and
mahogany bar-counters are
well-preserved although its interior
otherwise is a mixture of re-used
old fittings and imported new work.
Changes in 1970 opened the bottom tap
room through to the middle lounge – via
steps through a former chimney breast –
and blocked the latter's side-street
entrance. (Closed Sunday evenings.)

77

Huddersfield (central)
1 St John's Road, HD1 5AY
Unlisted
LPA: Kirklees 🔲 ⇌ 🍺

Sportsman

The Sportsman is an interesting combination of original 1930 build (by local brewer Seth Senior), 1950s refitting (by Hammond's of Bradford, whose logo appears in the windows) and 2009 revamp by its new private owners. The Thirties influence is strongest in the smoke room, tap room and the intact gents' (which has good sporting theme tiling) while the main lounge has banquette seating in bays and a bar with sweeping canopy, fluted pilasters and glass shelving – all in classic Fifties mode. The latest refurbishment has brought some careful replacement and remodelling and a modern décor that might have been equally at home in the 1950s.

The main lounge of the Sportsman, Huddersfield with its modern makeover.

Further illustration: **page 89 (tile detail)**

Huddersfield (Lockwood)
11 Neale Road, HD1 3TN
(01484) 424835
Unlisted
LPA: Kirklees 🍺

Shoulder of Mutton

Forming part of a characterful little enclave of gritstone buildings, the Shoulder was extensively reconstructed in 1927 by the Lockwood Estate, its then owners. It preserves two very good front rooms from that time, either side of a tiled entrance lobby and both with quality fitted seating: one is an intimate parlour, the other has glazed and leaded screenwork (which is echoed in the new outside windows). These rooms were, astonishingly, suggested for opening-up in 2006 but saved, thanks to the licensee. Elsewhere inside, the removal of a snug has lost some of the integrity of the 1927 scheme but the rear lounge, with its semi-octagonal bar, retains some original fittings.

Huddersfield (Newsome)
105 Jackroyd Lane, HD4 6RB
Unlisted
LPA: Kirklees

Victoria

This 1935 suburban house, locally nicknamed 'The Bum', is sited high-up towards Huddersfield's landmark Victoria Tower and was ingeniously designed for its corner site by local architects Joseph Berry & Sons for the Sheffield brewer William Stones. It has a quite intriguing layout of two wings pivoting on an octagonal smoke room at the corner angle. One wing features a hall-lounge and a former 'refreshment room' (now largely merged together) and the other has an offsales department (now kitchen) and a tap room. A triangular servery completes the geometry, with a curved bar-counter fronting to the lounge-hall. Both entrance porches are later accretions.

Kirkheaton
Church Lane, HD5 0BH
(01484) 517777
Grade II listed
LPA: Kirklees

Beaumont Arms (Kirkstile)

A high quality Tudor-style refurbishment by Joshua Tetley & Son, soon after they acquired this premises in 1935, has left an impressive legacy of joinery work, especially on the staircase, and robust fitted seating, good brick fireplaces and restrained glasswork in the main lounges and function room. Tetley's themselves went on to preside over increments of post-war change here, including considerable opening-up, but they made efforts to match the quality of the older work – and indeed declared this one of their 'Heritage Inns' in 1989.

Ledsham
Claypit Lane, LS25 5LP
(01977) 683135
Unlisted
LPA: Leeds

Chequers

Attractive stone village pub belonging to a country estate. Its interior has a sense of age-old rambling character but much of it derives from a major refit of 1962, partly done in the heavy-timber and exposed-stone idiom (which became a fashion for 'destination' pubs) of which this is a good early example. The revamp created the present servery and counters, blocked the old pub entrance, and started the process of adding more rooms (to the original two) while showing admirable concern for maintaining compartmented character.

YORKSHIRE'S REAL HERITAGE PUBS

Leeds (central)

3–5 Hunslet Road, Leeds Bridge, LS10 1JQ

(0113) 245 6377

Grade II listed

LPA: Leeds 🄲 ⇌ 🍺

Adelphi ★

Built 1901 in the majestic style of a high-Victorian drinking 'palace' (few of this type were ever built in Yorkshire's cities) the Adelphi was designed by Leeds architect Thomas Winn for the local Melbourne Brewery. Its highly-ornate, multi-roomed interior was carefully looked after for many years by Melbourne's powerful successor, Joshua Tetley & Son, and it has survived wonderfully well (although the effect has been superficially offset of late by some 'café-bar' décor). Four spacious rooms open off a drinking foyer from which a lavish staircase rises grandly to a former ballroom, and there is a rich array of original tiling, etched glasswork and mahogany fittings on display. The sub-division of the large public bar with a sympathetically designed screen was done by Tetley's in the 1980s – the same decade that they gave the Adelphi the special recognition of their 'Heritage' badging (in 1983). Statutorily listed in 1998 following CAMRA's Leeds pilot study for English Heritage.

Leeds (central)

2 Templar Street (corner Vicar Lane) LS2 7NU

(0113) 243 0318

Unlisted   LPA: Leeds 🍺

Templar. The tiled exterior and some quality 'Tudor' elements are what remain from a 1927 design scheme for Melbourne brewery by Pontefract architects Garside & Pennington. The chief interest is the back lounge, which was largely unaffected by a re-modelling that opened out the main body of pub in the mid-1980s.

Leeds (central)

Turk's Head Yard, Briggate,
LS1 6HB
(0113) 245 3950
Grade II listed
LPA: Leeds

Whitelock's ★

Described by John Betjeman as
"the very heart of Leeds", Whitelock's
was once like nothing else in this region:
one of that special breed of old-style
luncheon bars that only a few of the UK's

biggest cities could boast.
Tucked away up an old alley,
it has been licensed since 1715 but the pub of today is
essentially late Victorian – the result of a major re-modelling
in 1895 by local architects Waite & Sons for the Whitelock
family, its owners from 1880. A combination of long, narrow
plan-form (reflecting the plot's medieval origins), dark wood
panelling, glittering copper and brasswork, plus a rich display
of old mirrors, creates a unique environment that has
changed little in over 100 years. The tile-fronted bar-counter,
topped partly in marble, partly in copper, is a rarity in itself.
The seating areas, divided into shallow bays with ceiling-
high brass posts were part of the Victorian scheme as were,
probably, the colourful leaded windows. Whitelock's has a
history of association with the world of the arts and enjoyed

Pre-war heyday at Whitelock's.
Its renowned 'mine host', Lupton
Whitelock (seated left) is pictured here
in 1938, entertaining Yorkshire and
England cricketing legend Len Hutton.
(Photo by kind courtesy of Sarah Whitelock)

a golden age in the 1930s. It continues today in its busy role as a pub
and eating place, although the rear section is no longer presented as
the separate and distinctive dining area it once was. The 'Top Bar',
further up the yard, is a modern conversion, dating only from the 1980s.

Below: **The main interior of Whitelock's.**

81

Leeds (Burley)
364 Kirkstall Road, LS4 2HQ
Grade II listed
LPA: Leeds 🍺

Right: Right: the central lobby
Below: the front smoke room,
looking through to the central lobby.

Cardigan Arms ★

Built in 1896 with an eye on the affluent new housing developments of Lord Cardigan's Leeds estates, the 'Cardy' is outstanding for the overall completeness of its compartmented interior. With four rooms of different sizes off a large L-shaped drinking lobby, a separate vaults (formerly sub-divided with a 'Ladies Only' compartment) and an upstairs function room, it is the most internally complex of a surviving local trio of substantial Victorian pubs by Leeds architect Thomas Winn (q.v. the Adelphi [p. 80] and the Rising Sun [next entry below]). Winn's client here was a private individual – Benjamin Greaves,

a local entrepreneur with interests in some of the nearby housing. The pub's interior still preserves much of its as-built décor and fittings with extensive use made of etched glass, fine woodwork and ornamented ceilings and wall-coverings. There are also signs of a 1930s makeover – e.g. the

woodwork in the Oak Room and tiling in the right-hand corridor and the gents' – and the bar-fittings are from restoration work in the 1980s by its long-time owners, Joshua Tetley & Son, who gave this fine pub their 'Heritage' badging in1989. Statutorily listed in 1998 following CAMRA's Leeds pilot study for English Heritage. The old outbuildings include a (disused) tower brewhouse.

Leeds (Burley)
290 Kirkstall Road, LS4 2DN
Grade II listed
LPA: Leeds

Rising Sun ★ ⊗

Built *circa* 1899 for the local Melbourne Brewery, this is the least flamboyant of three Thomas Winn-designed drinking 'palaces' that have survived in Leeds (the others being the Adelphi [p.80] and the nearby Cardigan Arms [previous entry above]). A particular highlight is the imposing curved 'clerestory' screenwork that flanks the L-shaped corridor. The pub was given Tetley's 'Heritage' badging in 1989 and statutorily listed in 1998 following CAMRA's Leeds pilot study for English Heritage. Its fortunes declined and it traded for three years as a second-hand furniture shop before closing following a fire in 2013 (which, mercifully, spared the downstairs from undue damage)

Mosaic floor panel at entrance.

Leeds (Holbeck)
Back Row, Holbeck, LS11 5PL
(0113) 243 9254
Unlisted
LPA: Leeds ⇌ 🍺

Grove

Just a short walk from Leeds railway station and engulfed in a setting of towering modern high-rise, the Grove is a comforting reminder of a different age. Built around 1830, it has a very traditional 'corridor' plan but was, in fact, considerably re-modelled by John Smith's brewery in 1928/29, when the rear concert room was added. Much old bench seating remains, with an unusual bentwood type in the back snug, but features like the bar fittings are from a 1989 revamp and the doorway to the public bar has clearly been repositioned.

Leeds (Hunslet)
3 Whitfield Place, LS10 2QB
(0113) 277 7705
Grade II* listed
LPA: Leeds 🍺

Garden Gate ★

Probably the 'jewel in the crown' of historic pub architecture in Yorkshire, the Garden Gate is a treasure house of Edwardian decorative design. Apart from the loss of its original off-sales (on the right) the layout and internal fittings of this marvellous pub are virtually untouched since 1902–3 when it was rebuilt for its private owner by Stourton architect W. Mason Coggill. It combines a very traditional small-pub layout (central through corridor, counter in the vault, and hatch service to other rooms) with resplendent decoration, inside and out, to rival the great city drinking 'palaces' of the period. Its riches include etched glass with Art Nouveau motifs, lavish tiling, mosaic floors, moulded plasterwork and ornate mahogany fitments. Much of the glazed ceramic work would be from Leeds' renowned Burmantofts Company and another local firm, J Claughton, had a major hand in the internal furnishing, as their fitters' labels in the back-left lounge clearly testify. The undoubted highlight is the vaults, a veritable *tour de force* of the decorative tiler's art which centres on a magnificent curved ceramic bar-counter and elaborate mahogany back-fitting. The Garden Gate was one of the first on Tetley's list for 'Heritage' badging in 1983, yet it is a sobering thought that, but for action by enlightened local protesters a decade earlier, this historic gem would have been lost forever to an urban clearance scheme. Positive developments in 2010 were its upgrading to II* listing, following a successful application by CAMRA, and its purchase by the local Leeds Brewery.

Faience fire surround (*above*) and Art Nouveau glasswork (*top*) at the Garden Gate.
Right: the back smoke room.

Further illustrations: front cover (the splendid vaults), page 13 (corridor) and page 69 (exterior).

Leeds (Hunslet)
93 Moor Road, LS10 1JJ
(0113) 270 5175
Unlisted
LPA: Leeds 🍺

Prospect

An unpretentious but highly-regarded working local which has barely altered since the 1950s and combines characteristics of that era, like the seating and bar in the right-hand lounge, with internal doors and entrance lobby from a 1920s refit – all by John Smith's Tadcaster Brewery who acquired the Prospect around 1924. Their 1950s alterations elongated the vaults (into a former kitchen) and converted a former front-right smoke room into toilets. The '1822' gable datestone outside belonged to former workshops on the site.

Leeds (Woodhouse)
161 Woodhouse Lane, LS2 3ED
Unlisted
LPA: Leeds 🔘 🍺

Fenton. Except for the opening-through of its left-side rooms, the Fenton preserves its original planning, with dog-legging corridor/lobby and excellent glazed corridor-screen as hallmark features. It also retains some old seating but most other fittings and finishes are late twentieth century replacements. Rare Tetley lantern sign outside.

Leeds (Woodhouse)
208 Woodhouse Lane, LS2 9DX
(0113) 245 3980
Grade II listed
LPA: Leeds 🍺

Pack Horse

A purpose-designed, brick-built Victorian public house of 1871. Its traditional 'corridor' layout is well-preserved and the small rooms to either side – tap room to left and two lounges to the right – retain their fitted seating with nicely-fashioned armrests and bell-pushes. Other Victorian fittings and finishes include terrazzo flooring, wood-lined walls, panelled bar-front and tiled fireplaces. The back lounge area was once screened off by glazed partitioning. Statutorily listed in 1994 following CAMRA's Leeds pilot study for English Heritage.

Leeds (Wortley)
8 Tong Road, LS12 1HX
Grade II listed
LPA: Leeds

Beech ★ ⊗

This is the last substantial survivor of a dozen or so newbuilds that were produced by the local Melbourne Brewery between the Wars. Almost all of them were to designs, as here, by the Pontefract architects Garside & Pennington. Built in 1931, the Beech's interesting original

Beech: the front vaults.

Further illustrations: page 70
('Melbourne' window and signage)

layout (of spacious front vaults, with smoke room and club room in tandem arrangement behind) is unaltered, as are many of its internal fittings and finishes, while outside are some well-preserved examples of old Melbourne livery and signage. It was statutorily listed in 2010 following a successful application by CAMRA and remains intact, but it has been closed since 2011, prompting fears for its future.

Leeds (Wortley)
65 Lower Wortley Road,
LS12 4SL
Unlisted
LPA: Leeds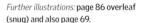

Hanover Arms

Opened in 1940, the Hanover was a high-quality newbuild by John Smith's Tadcaster Brewery, designed by their company architect Bertram Wilson in the style of a spacious Jacobean country house. The quality of the original scheme can still be appreciated in the décor and fittings of the excellent foyer-lounge ('Blue Room') and in the toilets, both sets of which are impressively authentic and intact. Little else, though, has escaped a degree of post-war revamping and the merging of the tap room and old off-sales is as recent as 2005.

Northowram
1 Mutton Fold, Towngate, HX3 7EA
(01422) 206229
Grade II listed
LPA: Calderdale

Shoulder of Mutton. The main interest here is the rear tap room which has matchboarded ceiling, tiled arched fireplace and what must surely be some of the oldest wooden bench seating surviving in any pub today. Despite its present rather neglected state, this room is a potential treasure and deserves restoration.

Norwood Green
Village Street, HX3 8QG
(01274) 676645
Grade II listed
LPA: Calderdale

Further illustrations: **page 86 overleaf** (snug) and also page 69.

Olde White Beare ★

The old snug here is surely one of the best historic pub rooms to be found anywhere in England. With its high-backed settles, old stone fireplace and low-beamed ceiling, and divided-off by matchboard partitions (partly curving and partly top-glazed for borrowed light) it is a little gem. This remarkable survival is set inside a country 'destination' pub which enjoys great popularity with diners and which, although most pleasant, has undergone its share of modern

Snug interior, Olde White Beare, Norwood Green.

change. It has few other fittings or features of historic note. In latter years it has lost one of its former three drinking rooms, with new toilets replacing the old back tap room, while the main front bar-room has been considerably altered and modernised. The counter here, for instance, dates from around 2000.

Otley
Newall Carr Road, LS21 2AU
(01943) 461330
Unlisted
LPA: Leeds

Yew Tree. Converted from an old farmhouse by Tetley's brewery in 1974, this is the 'youngest' entry in our listings but an unusually complete example of its kind – with simple, traditional plan of public bar and lounge (both with banquette seating and dark wood fittings), central servery and an entrance lobby with hatch for outdoor service.

Pudsey
30 Station Street, LS28 8PR
(0113) 256 5007   Unlisted
LPA: Leeds

Royal

On a site overlooking Pudsey Greenside railway station (now long-gone) the Royal was built in 1879, the same year as the station, and has the imposing look of a small Victorian railway hotel. It was extensively

revamped in 1936 by the Bradford brewers William Whitaker & Sons whose re-modelling created an enlarged vaults, an off-sales, and the servery arrangement we see today. The two left hand rooms were retained but refitted in Thirties style. Post-war alterations have removed the off-sales (now absorbed into the vaults) and brought a degree of opening-up, but Thirties character is still evident, not least in the light oak joinery, seating and terrazzo floors.

The vaults at the Royal, Pudsey

Pudsey
2 Hough Side Road, LS28 9BR
Unlisted
LPA: Leeds 🍺

White Horse. Surprisingly little-altered (apart from the refitted servery) from the plans submitted by Tetley's brewery in 1938 which adapted the pub's old 'corridor' layout and created its present open-plan core. The two small front rooms, flanking the front entrance, are reminders of the older layout and have their original seating.

Shipley
3 Bradford Road, BD18 3PR
(01274) 584386
Unlisted
LPA: Bradford ⇌ 🍺

Ring O'Bells

Suburban Edwardian pub whose smoke room, separated-off just beyond an open staircase, is the last surviving complete room in an interior which once had six. This little room boasts high quality fitted seating with carved armrests and has its original etched door and window glass (the fireplace is more recent). Elsewhere, despite all the opening-up, the pub's rich array of window decoration (some of it repro), its ceilings and its good fitted seating are worthwhile reminders of its former splendour.

Sowerby Bridge
Burnley Road, Friendly, HX6 2UG
(01422) 831173
Unlisted
LPA: Calderdale 🍺

White Horse

An intact refurbishment of 1962 which is an example of good late work by the Halifax brewers Ramsden's. Designed by their managing director, T Hardy, a qualified architect, the scheme re-fashioned the older premises here into a practical two-room interior, unfussy but with quality features. The servery has the clean lines redolent of its time, with fine wood finishes, recessed lighting and mirror-backed shelving. Both rooms have fitted seating and the neat tap room is served by hatch. The lounge-bar's plasterwork has pyramid motifs.

87

Wakefield (central)
28 Horbury Road, WF2 8TS
Unlisted
LPA: Wakefield
⇌ (Westgate) 🍺

Redoubt

A good old corridor-centred pub which evolved out of vernacular stone cottages. What stands out here is the authentic layout, the old back-left lounge and, above all, the splendidly-unaltered tap room (still with its 'Gents Only' sign from the not-so-distant past!). Tetley's, the pub's owners for more than a century, gave the Redoubt their 'Heritage' badging in 1985 but went on to completely refit the servery, including enlargement of the corridor hatch. The decorative windows to the front bar are also their late 20th century work.

Right: **The Redoubt's tap room.**

Wakefield (Eastmoor)
Barden Road, WF1 4HP
Unlisted
LPA: Wakefield

Rocking Horse ⊗

Purpose-built by Tetley's in 1955 for the big surrounding council estates, this is one of few known examples of its kind in Yorkshire to survive so intact. Designed by Kitson, Parish, Ledgard & Pyman, the Leeds architects long-associated with Tetley's, it has something of a pre-war flavour and original joinery in an attractive light oak. Its symmetrical layout has tap room and lounge either side of a central servery, a connecting back lobby, and a projecting front pod containing the room entrance porches and the (defunct) off-sales.

Rocking Horse: the lounge.

Appendix A
Architectural ceramics in Yorkshire's pubs

Of the decorative materials that are most associated with Victorian and Edwardian public houses, architectural ceramics – the various building products that are made of fired clay – have often been the longest-lasting. Yorkshire preserves some excellent examples of their use and Yorkshire was also the home of the Burmantofts Company, the Leeds-based firm which was one of the country's largest and most important manufacturers, rivalling famous names like Doulton for markets throughout the UK and overseas.

Ceramics offered great scope for flamboyant decoration and this, combined with the practical advantages of durability, ease of cleaning and high resistance to sooty atmospheres, meant these products held a ready appeal for pub architects working in the big grimy cities like Leeds, Sheffield, Hull and Middlesbrough.

For internal work, moulded components in faience (the multi-coloured glazed version of terracotta) were often used in combination with elaborate tiling – to outstanding effect at the Garden Gate, Leeds and the Zetland, Middlesbrough, two pubs with floor-to-ceiling tiled rooms that are among the finest in the land. The Garden Gate also boasts a superb original ceramic bar counter, one of only fourteen now left in the whole UK, a distinction it shares with three other Yorkshire pubs – Whitelock's, also in Leeds, and the Polar Bear and the White Hart in Hull. (The Golden Ball, York has a rare tiled counter-front too, this time

of the inter-war period). Original ceramics can be found in a good many of the other pubs in this guide, but chiefly confined to tiled dados and mosaic floors in entrance lobbies and hallways, with faience also featuring in the wall claddings and sometimes in fire surrounds. A few pub toilets too preserve original ceramic work and examples like the 1930s pictorial 'sporting theme' tiles in the gents' at the Sportsman, Huddersfield (*above*) are now rarities of special note.

For exteriors, the use of ceramics was rivalling stone by the end of the nineteenth century, whether in its unglazed terracotta or faience form. A good deal of this work still survives, much of it on pubs with ruined interiors, but three of the most spectacular facades are on premises that also feature in this guide – notably the Alexandra and the Windmill in Hull and, again, the Garden Gate, Leeds. Firms like Burmantofts also developed matt-glazed products like their 'Marmo' (resembling marble) for yet more design versatility and, by the 1930s, such facings were common in the modest 'Art Deco'-influenced house styles adopted by brewers like Gilmour's of Sheffield and Melbourne of Leeds.

Appendix B
The Selection Criteria for CAMRA's Inventories

What really matters about a pub is its interior. CAMRA's inventories of historic pub interiors focus entirely on the *internal physical fabric* of pubs and what is *authentically old* inside them. In this context a pub's external architecture, fine though it may be, is a side issue.

National or regional significance?
The pubs that qualify for the National Inventory (NI) must have outstanding attributes – either a high degree of internal intactness or, where there has been alteration, some truly exceptional features or rooms. Outstanding bars and pub-type rooms in other kinds of establishment, such as hotel bars, theatre bars or railway buffets, are also embraced. Rather less is expected of candidates for a regional inventory (RI), although they must retain a significant amount of genuine historic features and/or a good sense of their historic layout. Most pubs included on an RI will have some combination of both.

Age
The main focus of CAMRA's inventories is on pre-1939 interiors – fabric that is much as it was before the Second World War – but some later interiors that have survived unaltered, especially from before the mid-1960s (when the modern orgy of pub refitting and opening-out began in earnest) are now rare and have to be seriously considered too. There is, however, a need for more research to develop appropriate criteria for post-war pubs, and CAMRA is actively pursuing this, with help from York University and in parallel with current work being done by English Heritage. Meanwhile, CAMRA is careful to restrict its present selections to clear cases that have special merit (exceptional merit, in the case of the NI). Interiors later than 1970 do not qualify at all for the NI.

Historic pub fittings, features and plan-form
The emphasis is on items that reflect the premises' historic function *as a pub*, rather than inherited from some other (usually domestic) use of the building, although the line is not always easy to draw. Items of specific interest include such things as fixed settles or bench seating, bar-fittings (counter, bar-back),

screen partitioning, bell-pushes, dispense equipment and original toilets as well as fittings and décor purpose-designed for pubs (most famously by the Victorians and Edwardians, in decorative glass, joinery, plaster and ceramic work). If features like these survive in abundance, with little lost, the pub is a clear candidate for the NI.

The survival of historic layout is also a crucial factor in assessing NI candidates, but regional inventory candidates too should retain sufficient for their original internal planning to be appreciated and understood. Where a pub has undergone modern extension, as so many have, this need not count against it providing the work has been sensitively done (preferably kept physically separate) and does not seriously compromise its 'historic core'.

The bottom line?
If all that's left is a couple of fixed benches and a bit of matchboard panelling in a largely opened-up pub, inclusion will not be justified as these are commonplace and can be found in large numbers. Many pub interiors too still have a few old features like etched glass or tilework which are irreplaceable and a joy to behold but CAMRA has been cautious about developing plans for a nationally-led campaign to identify and catalogue them – the hope being that the inspiration for compiling such 'local inventories' will take off at the local level itself. Starting in 2014, however, CAMRA has embarked on two 'pilots', both in Yorkshire (in Barnsley and Sheffield) to serve as exemplars and to give a positive impetus to the whole process.

Factual evidence and informed judgement
CAMRA's inventories set great store by including only what is genuinely old. This ought to be a matter of objective, provable fact and certainly the selections for the Yorkshire Regional Inventory have been authenticated wherever possible from documentary sources like original plans, building records or other archive material. However, where no such material exists, as is often the case, the truth is not always easy to establish. Oral testimony from licensees and older regulars can be an invaluable help but reliance often has to be placed on experience and informed judgement.

Appendix C
The Yorkshire Regional Inventory, statutory and local listing

More than 700 pub buildings in Yorkshire & Humber are statutorily 'listed' in recognition of their 'special architectural and historic interest'. Most of them have been listed for reasons that have nothing whatsoever to do with their interiors, such as their fine external appearance, their contribution to historic townscape or, quite simply, their great age. The majority are wrecked internally and therefore find no place in CAMRA's inventories.

The fact of the matter is that interiors received little serious attention for years. It is only as recently as 1994 that English Heritage (the Government agency for the historic environment in England) published specific listing guidelines for public houses – *Pubs: Understanding Listing* – and brought some official emphasis at long last to the importance of interiors. CAMRA was an invited partner in the review which led up to this and contributed five detailed pilot studies, three of them in Yorkshire – for Harrogate, Leeds and York. Eight fresh listings of pubs in Leeds and York followed as a direct result.

Just over half our Yorkshire inventory pubs *are* in listed buildings, however, and this means that if changes are planned to any part of them, including their internal fixtures and fittings, listed building consent must be obtained from the local planning authority. Most of these (in common with 94% of listed buildings nationally) are listed at Grade II but five are placed higher, at Grade II*. This grading is reserved for buildings of exceptional importance and means English Heritage themselves will normally have a strong say in what changes are allowed. Information on its statutory listing status is given against each entry in this guide and, where CAMRA has been instrumental or involved in the application process, this is noted too.

For the other half of our Inventory entries, which lack the benefit of listing protection, there is much catching up to do. The point was made strongly in our Yorkshire consultation exercise and English Heritage responded positively by inviting applications for the unlisted Yorkshire pubs which also feature on CAMRA's National Inventory – i.e. the candidates most likely to meet their current strict criteria. The welcome outcome was five fresh listings in 2010, all of pubs with important inter-war interiors, and the upgrading of the Garden Gate in Leeds to II*.

At the same time, other listing applications for inventory pubs were turned down, indicating that some of our important surviving pub interiors did not yet, and possibly may never, satisfy the national listing criteria. This, in its way, only adds strength to our argument for *an independent statement of pub preservation priorities, alongside and in addition to statutory listing* – which is exactly what CAMRA's inventories provide.

CAMRA firmly believes that all the pubs on the Yorkshire Regional Inventory are worthy of protection and sensitive treatment. Where statutory listing is lacking, or unlikely to be forthcoming we would very much like see these pubs added to a 'local list' of historic buildings. Some of the local planning authorities responding to our Yorkshire consultation undertook to do just this, although there are still only three of them with active schemes in operation at the present time (2014). Despite having no legal force, local lists raise awareness of the local historic environment and can be an extra lever in encouraging would-be developers to look after their pubs sympathetically, thus saving them expense and preserving an asset for the community.

Appendix D
Consultation for the Yorkshire Regional Inventory

Formal consultation for the *Yorkshire Regional Inventory of Historic Pub Interiors* was launched in December 2007 and was kept open until 2009. Detailed documentation went to all the principal consultees (including separately-addressed mailings to chief planners and heads of conservation in all the region's planning authorities) and a temporary website was specially set up for the exercise. The representative bodies consulted, including the professional associations, all willingly co-operated by extending the consultation to their entire memberships – through internal newsletters, email networks and websites – and some of the numbers involved in this wider reach are noted below.

The principal parties contacted and invited to contribute were as follows:

The local planning authorities
Barnsley Metropolitan Borough Council
City of Bradford Metropolitan District Council
City of York Council
Calderdale Metropolitan Borough Council
Craven District Council
Doncaster Metropolitan Borough Council
East Riding of Yorkshire Council
Hambleton District Council
Harrogate Borough Council
Kingston upon Hull City Council
Kirklees Council
Leeds City Council
North York Moors National Park Authority
North Lincolnshire Council
North East Lincolnshire Council
North Yorkshire County Council
Peak District National Park Authority
Richmondshire District Council
Rotherham Metropolitan Borough Council
Ryedale District Council
Scarborough Borough Council
Selby District Council
Sheffield City Council
Wakefield Council
Yorkshire Dales National Park Authority

Local civic and amenity societies
Barnsley Civic Trust
Beverley Civic Society
Doncaster Civic Trust
Grimsby, Cleethorpes & District Civic Society
Halifax Civic Trust
Harrogate Civic Society
Hull Civic Society
Huddersfield Civic Society
Leeds Civic Trust
Rotherham Civic Society
Scarborough & District Civic Society
Sheffield Civic Trust
Wakefield Civic Trust
York Civic Trust

Professional associations for the built environment
Institute of Historic Building Conservation
    (1,700 national members)
Royal Institute of British Architects , Yorkshire
    (2,500 regional members)
Royal Institute of Chartered Surveyors ,Yorkshire
    (6,000 regional members)
Royal Town Planning Institute, Yorkshire
    (1,350 regional members)

Other bodies with built-environment or building preservation interests
Centre for Conservation Studies, University of York
Council for British Archaeology, Yorkshire
    (1,500 national contacts)
Dept of Architecture, Landscape and Design,
    Leeds Metropolitan University
English Heritage, Yorkshire & Humber
English Heritage, North: Heritage Protection
Museums, Libraries and Archives, Yorkshire
Victorian Society, South Yorkshire Regional Group
Victorian Society, West Yorkshire Regional Group
Yorkshire & Humberside Association of Civic Societies
    (75 societies)
Yorkshire Culture / Y&H Historic Environment Forum
    (21 organisations)

Yorkshire Local Councils Association
(400 parish councils)
Yorkshire Vernacular Buildings Study Group
(240 members)

Pub industry and pub promotion bodies
British Beer & Pubs Association, North (28 companies)
Pub is the Hub

Pub-owning and operating companies
Admiral Taverns
Enterprise Inns
Marston's Pub Company

Mitchells & Butlers
Pub People Company
Punch Taverns
Samuel Smith Old Brewery (Tadcaster)
Scottish & Newcastle Pub Enterprises
Daniel Thwaites

Yorkshire MPs with a known special interest in pubs issues
John Grogan, Selby (then Chair, All Party
Parliamentary Beer Group)
Greg Mulholland, Leeds North West (Chair, All Party
Parliamentary Save the Pub Group)

Editor's acknowledgements

'Yorkshire's Real Heritage Pubs', a labour of love, builds on many hours of careful work by a small number of dedicated volunteers: Alan Canvess, Geoff Henman, Peter Robinson, Allan Sykes and John Thornton have been the ever-present core of the Yorkshire Regional Inventory team since the mid-1990s, and the Editor owes them, and other close CAMRA colleagues, a great debt of gratitude for their ever-willing help and support. The gratitude extends to Robert Anderson, an early member of the team, to Jim Sambrooks, Mick Moss and Kevin Keaveny who joined it later, to Stuart Mumby and Dave Pickersgill for their more recent active involvement and to others in the Yorkshire branches who have willingly provided information for this Revised Edition. For their particular help with the book's preparation I am indebted to my Pub Heritage Group colleagues Paul Ainsworth, Mick Slaughter and Geoff Brandwood: Paul, for cheerfully acting as critic and wise sounding-board for the revised texts, Mick for his immense and generous help with the photographic material, and Geoff for some excellent new photographs. A special word here too for Paul Thompson, a professional photographer who has given generously, and voluntarily, of his time and skills to provide fresh pictures; and mention too for my partner, Jean Scott, for her patient support and her proof-reading.

The acknowledgements and thanks expressed in the First Edition, moreoever, are no less sincere for repetition here: to Andrew Davison and Mike Mackintosh, colleagues from the earliest days of CAMRA in York, whose background contributions were invaluable in the first writing of the guide; to my late friend, George Williamson, for all the knowledgeable insights he provided; and to the many people outside CAMRA who have helped or contributed in their different ways to the Inventory project, with special mention to Nick Bridgland of English Heritage, to Lee LeClerq of the BBPA, to the late Chris Ketchell of Hull Local History Unit, to Jim Brettell of Leeds Civic Trust and to Mr Humphrey Smith of Samuel Smith's Brewery.

Finally a very sincere thanks must go to the people at the production end of this Revised Edition; to Simon Hall and Katie Button at CAMRA head office for their constructive support and to Dale Tomlinson who, for his cheerful, ever-obliging attitude and his professional skill, has once again been an absolute joy to work with.

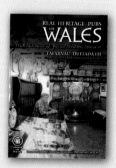

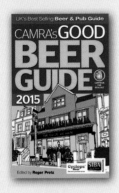

Good Beer Guide 2015
Edited by **ROGER PROTZ**

The original independent guide to good beer and good pubs. You're never far from a great pint with the *Good Beer Guide* to hand. Now in its 42nd edition, the fully revised and updated Guide recommends pubs in England, Wales, Scotland, Northern Ireland and offshore islands that serve the best real ale. From country inns through urban style bars to backstreet boozers – if you love pubs, don't leave home without the *Good Beer Guide*.

£15.99   ISBN 978 1 85249 320 2

Good Bottled Beer Guide
JEFF EVANS

A pocket-sized guide for discerning drinkers looking to buy bottled real ales and enjoy a fresh glass of their favourite beers at home. The 8th edition of the *Good Bottled Beer Guide* is completely revised, updated and redesigned to showcase the very best bottled British real ales now being produced, and detail where they can be bought. Everything you need to know about bottled beers; tasting notes, ingredients, brewery details, and a glossary to help the reader understand more about them.

£12.99   ISBN 978 1 85249 309 7

Britain's Beer Revolution
ROGER PROTZ and **ADRIAN TIERNEY-JONES**

UK brewing has seen unprecedented growth in the last decade. Breweries of all shapes and sizes are flourishing. Established brewers applying generations of tradition in new ways rub shoulders at the bar with new micro-brewers. Headed by real ale, a 'craft' beer revolution is sweeping the country. In *Britain's Beer Revolution* Roger Protz and Adrian Tierney-Jones look behind the beer labels and shine a spotlight on what makes British beer so good.

£14.99   ISBN 978 1 85249 321 9

Order these and other CAMRA books online at **www.camra.org.uk/books**, *ask your local bookstore, or contact*: CAMRA, 230 Hatfield Road, St Albans, AL1 4LW. *Telephone* 01727 867201

A Campaign of Two Halves

Campaigning for Pub Goers & Beer Drinkers

CAMRA, the Campaign for Real Ale, is the not-for-profit independent voice of real ale drinkers and pub goers. CAMRA's vision is to have quality real ale and thriving pubs in every community. We campaign tirelessly to achieve this goal, as well as lobbying government to champion drinkers' rights. As a CAMRA member you will have the opportunity to campaign to save pubs under threat of closure, for pubs to be free to serve a range of real ales at fair prices and for a long term freeze in beer duty that will help Britain's brewing industry survive.

Enjoying Real Ale & Pubs

CAMRA has over 165,000 members from all ages and backgrounds, brought together by a common belief in the issues that CAMRA deals with and their love of good quality British beer. From just £23 a year* – that's less than a pint a month – you can join CAMRA and enjoy the following benefits:

Subscription to *What's Brewing*, our monthly colour newspaper, and *Beer*, our quarterly magazine, informing you about beer and pub news and detailing events and beer festivals around the country.

Free or reduced entry to over 160 national, regional and local beer festivals.

Money off many of our publications including the *Good Beer Guide*, the *Good Bottled Beer Guide* and *Britain's Best Real Heritage Pubs*.

Access to a members-only section of our national website, **www.camra.org.uk**, which gives up-to-the-minute news stories and includes a special offer section with regular features.

Special discounts with numerous partner organisations and money off real ale in your participating local pubs as part of our Pubs Discount Scheme.

Log onto **www.camra.org.uk/joinus** for CAMRA membership information.

CAMPAIGN
FOR
REAL ALE

*£23 membership cost stated is only available via Direct Debit, other concessionary rates available. Please note membership rates stated are correct at the time of printing but are subject to change. Full details of all membership rates can be found here: www.camra.org.uk/membershiprates